Read & Listen

S Forsyth T Bacciarelli A Forsyth
J Ward

Oliver & Boyd

Acknowledgements

The authors and publishers are grateful to the following for illustrations and the use of photographs:

Vince Reid, David Mostyn, Barry Wilkinson, Bob Geary, Shirley Tourret, Steven Gibson and John Marshall.

Ardea Photographics p. 11; Keystone pp. 62, 63, 64; National Film Archive p. 63; Popperfoto p. 44; Sally Ann Thompson p. 70; Topham Picture Library p. 52; Universal Pictorial Press pp. 49, 56.

The authors and publishers are grateful to the following for the use of copyright material:

Michael Joseph Ltd. for extract from *Kestrel for a Knave* by Barry Hines; Jennifer Luithlen Agency for extract from *Saucers Over the Moon* by Malcolm Saville; Lutterworth Press for extract from *The Sea Falcon* by Erroll Collins from *Boy's Own Annual 1940/41; The Observer* for extract from *The Observer Magazine,* May 1985; Laurence Pollinger Ltd and the Estate of Mrs Frieda Lawrence Ravagli for extract from *Adolph* by D. H. Lawrence from *The Complete Short Stories of D. H. Lawrence;* Times Newspapers Ltd for *The Britain I Knew* by Tom Mboya from *The Sunday Times Magazine,* February 1963; *The Talking Shop of the World* by Trevor Fishlock from *The Times,* October 1985 © Times Newspapers, 1985.

Oliver & Boyd
Robert Stevenson House
1–3 Baxter's Place
Leith Walk
Edinburgh EH1 3BB

A Division of Longman Group UK Ltd

ISBN 0 05 004048 0
First published 1989

Set in Univers Light 10/12pt and Optima 10/12pt (Linotron 202)
Produced by Longman Group (FE) Ltd
Printed in Hong Kong

Contents

INTRODUCTION

Your Reading Skills

Most students *assume* they can read – after all, they've been doing it for years. But in fact, reading something to absorb the sense and grasp the significance and implications of what's printed in front of you, is a complex business, involving a whole battery of skills. But obviously such skills, like any other skills, can be developed, sharpened, both by *awareness* of what they are and *practice* of their use. The basic purpose of this book is to make you aware of the skills you possess, in differing degrees of 'sharpness', and to provide opportunities for you to exercise them.

When your reading is tested by questions set on a given passage, the questions, in effect, are really requiring you to demonstrate that you have such skills, and to what level you have them.

It is worth noting straight away that the skills demanded by the wide range of questions set by teachers and examiners come under *four* main headings. Each heading denotes one of the key stages that might be involved in understanding what you read. Let's consider this process.

1) Identification

First of all, a question directs you, in some way, to find the *relevant* part of the passage which contains the answer to the question. In other words, you've got to *identify* the right bit! This might mean you have to identify a particular word or expression, a piece of factual information, a statement, idea, punctuation mark, figurative device. But stage one is simply **identification**.

2) Translation

Sadly, the world demands more from you than that you point your finger at the right bit and say, "There you are! That's the answer!" You have to write it down, and to show that you understand what you have read, you are usually required to *translate* it. This **translation** is stage two. You are most frequently asked to translate from the writer's words into your own

words, but you can also be required to translate from numbers, say, into words, the statistical to the verbal, from the figurative to the literal, from the particular to the general.

3) Collation

Sometimes, too, you have to find not just one bit of information but two or more. What such questions demand is that you link these two bits together in some way, to compare the two, add them up, as it were. This is called **collation**.

4) Deduction

Often you are asked to draw some sort of conclusion from the information the passage gives you. This, as any reader of Sherlock Holmes knows, is called **deduction**. And you can draw a conclusion from given information, from given ideas, from the writer's use of a particular word or expression.

A particular question might involve only one of these four stages, or all four. You might think, therefore, that the 'easy' questions might be the one-stage questions, and the 'hard' questions involve all four stages. This is not necessarily the case. You might have to go through all four stages, but each stage might be quite simple in itself.

The Four-Stage Process

To see for yourself how this works in action, read the following passage carefully. We will then analyse three possible questions for you, in terms of the four-stage process – **identification** . . . **translation** . . . **collation** . . . **deduction**.

Sam sank deeper into his chair, paper hat askew, blushing furiously, trying to avert his eyes. But Aunt Mabel was not to be deterred.

"Samuel," she repeated, "will recite. He reads poetry beautifully – with such feeling!"

Sam wished he was deaf and dumb. Sam wished he was dead. He stole a surreptitious glance at his cousins, Eric-'n-Ernie, then demolishing a fourth of ice-cream and jelly.

Eric-'n-Ernie, he knew, rated Kenny Dalgleish, they rated Man. United. In their First Division were Hammer Films, large dogs and Kung Fu. But poetry, he suspected, would rate somewhere in the relegation zone of Division Four. And boys who recited poetry – they would rate not at all.

And unfortunately, it was true. Sam did like poetry. He also liked magicians, and poets were magicians, pulling words and sounds and stories out of all sorts of unlikely hats. But such a weakness was not to be paraded before the incredulous eyes of such machoes as Eric-'n-Ernie. They looked at him curiously, their dessert spoons temporarily suspended.

"HORATIUS ON THE BRIDGE," said Aunt Mabel imperiously. "Come on, Samuel. Stand over here."

Question One

"What feeling controls Sam's actions in the first sentence?"

First of all, we identify the three actions – 'sank deeper into his chair', 'blushing furiously', 'trying to avert his eyes'.

In our minds we translate 'avert' = 'turn away'; we also translate each of the three actions. He sank deeper into his chair as if wanting to hide himself, to be as inconspicuous as possible, he blushed because he was embarrassed, he tried to avert his eyes to escape Aunt Mabel's eyes. We add all these up, we collate them, find the common factor, the main feeling. And we draw our conclusion. He did all of these things because he was embarrassed.

An easy enough question – but a complicated process.

Question Two

"Why are they all at Aunt Mabel's house?"

Of course, you know the answer. A party was going on. But how did you know? You identified 'paper hat' and 'ice-cream and jelly', collated these, and came up with the right conclusion. Easy? But if I then, as an examiner, asked for a *third* reason, that would make it a lot harder. I asked some students who were good at English to give me three reasons why they knew it was a party. They all said 'paper hat', they all said 'ice-cream and jelly' . . . . . but only about half of them said "A party . . because that's when some poor kid gets made to stand up and recite." Could *you* give a third reason?

Question Three

"Why does the writer write 'Eric-'n-Ernie' the way he does?"

Now, I would say this is a difficult question.

In the first place, can you identify what he has done?

1) He links the two names with dashes.
2) He starts both names with E.
3) He shortens 'and' into 'n', thus pulling the two names closer together. So when you collate them, you can see that he's really trying very hard to make the two of them almost into one. But why? Are they twins? Is he hinting that they are inseparable? Does he want us to think that the two of them are so alike – i.e. ordinary, healthy, pretty unsophisticated boys – as to be indistinguishable? All of these things? Something quite different?

Exercise

Try your hand at being the examiner, making up the questions. Make up three questions:

1) about what Eric-'n-Ernie like and admire,
2) about Aunt Mabel's character,
3) about why Sam likes poetry.

When you make up the questions, you must (a) give what you think is the correct answer, and (b) show clearly how the process of getting the answer *worked*.

Skills

On your behalf, we conducted a census, examining lots of exam questions teachers set, trying to work out what skills were tested, what skills, in fact, you were expected to possess. We eventually listed sixteen, and here they are.

1. Find a specific piece of factual information in the given passage.
2. Identify and collate two or more specific pieces of information in a given passage.
3. Translate such information into your own words.
4. Identify an *idea* in a passage.
5. Translate ideas into your own words.
6. Grasp the gist of a passage or story. (What's it about?)
7. Distinguish between primary and secondary information in a passage. (What's really important.)
8. Make inferences from given information. (Deduction?)
9. Identify the writer's purpose. (What's he getting at?)

10. Draw conclusions from writer's word choice as it influences *meaning*.
11. Draw conclusions from writer's word choice as it influences *tone*.
12. Relate the passage to your own experience.
13. Identify technical/figurative devices in the passage.
14. Respond to the writer's skill and purpose in using such devices.
15. Identify structural aspects of the passage. (How the passage as a whole is built up.)
16. Summarise narrative development/argument of the passage.

You will need the help of your teacher with this list of skills. We suggest that you don't need to 'master' this list of skills. You will come to understand just what they are as the course develops. Remember, *awareness* of what they are is a consequence of *practice* of their uses.

To start you thinking about them, here are questions on the passage given earlier about Sam and his cousins. Beside each question write down the number of the skill, (Nos. 1–16) mainly involved in answering the question. To do that, you have to think out what your answer would be and analyse how you arrived at that answer. Your teacher might suggest you do this exercise in small groups.

Questions

1. What relation was Eric to Sam?
2. Quote from the passage *two* pieces of information that suggest to you that Aunt Mabel was rather a domineering kind of person.
3. Explain clearly what each bit you have just quoted tells you about Aunt Mabel.
4. List any three of the things that Eric-'n-Ernie like and admire that help you to work out the meaning of 'machoes'.
5. HORATIUS ON THE BRIDGE is the title of a . . . . .
6. Aunt Mabel calls Sam 'Samuel'. Does this tell you anything about her character?
7. To what does Sam compare poets?
8. What is this figure of speech called?
9. Why does Sam think this is a good comparison? Do you agree with him?
10. Explain *fully* Sam's dilemma.
11. In your view, from what you have read in the passage, will Sam
    (a) stand up and recite?
    (b) refuse outright?
    (c) think of some excuse to get out of it?
    Give a reason for your answer.
12. Without making any reference to football whatsoever, explain what is implied by 'First Division', 'Division Four', 'relegation zone'.
13. Explain what is meant here by 'rate'.
14. What does the writer want us to understand by the words in italics:
    'spoons *temporarily* suspended'
    '*unfortunately*, it was true.'
15. Why does Sam wish, in paragraph two, that he were 'deaf', 'dumb', 'dead'?
16. Put these statements in the order in which they best seem to follow the order of the passage:

A. Although he thought personally that poetry was magic, he didn't want to recite and invite their contempt.
B. Aunt Mabel repeated her "invitation."
C. But Aunt Mabel was not going to let him off the hook.
D. Sam glanced at his cousins, remembering how they hated anything they considered 'unmanly'.
E. Sam curled up in acute embarrassment, desperately trying to become anonymous.

Note: There are 16 skills, 16 sample questions. *Don't* draw the obvious conclusion.

Conclusion

Finally, think of the three model questions we looked at – and the sixteen following questions. In your view, what were the *four* easiest questions, what were the *four* you found most difficult? Did all the class agree about these choices? Why were they easy? Why did you find others difficult?

Unit 1

Passages for close reading

Introductory Note

1) Here are 12 passages for close reading, with set questions to which suggested marks are attached.
2) The questions are grouped in 4 sections, each section demanding progressively subtler reading skills.
3) The suggested total mark for each passage is 40 marks.
4) The time suggested is approximately 1 hour.
5) Within that time allowance, and allowing some variation for the stage of the course when a passage is attempted, experience suggests that a Credit candidate should aggregate 21–24 marks, and a good Credit candidate a minimum of 28 marks.
   These are very approximate but perhaps helpful indicators.
6) Each passage also contains one 'boxed' question. This does *not* contribute to the overall 40 marks.

On a following page, each boxed question is analysed, a written answer is supplied, and the answer in turn is then analysed. In this way, reading skills are seen *in action* and *in context*.

To the Teacher:

Teachers are free to decide how to make best use of this device, but we have located them in this way to allow students to see them in context *as a question they might realistically have had to answer*, yet they are not overly intrusive to a student working on the passage at his/her own pace.

1 Dig Them Owls!

The hole we had found turned out to be some eight feet in length, curving slightly like the letter C, and about two feet at the greatest depth below the surface. We discovered all this by probing gently with a long and slender bamboo. Having marked out with sticks a rough plan of how the burrow lay, we proceeded to dig down, sinking a shaft into the tunnel at intervals of about two feet. Then each section of tunnel between the shafts was carefully searched to make sure nothing was hiding in it, and blocked off with clods of earth. At length we came to the final shaft, which, if our primitive reckoning was correct, should lead us down into the nesting chamber.

We worked in excited silence, gently chipping away the hard-baked soil. At intervals during our excavations we had pressed our ears to the turf, but there had been no sound from inside, and I was half convinced that the burrow would prove empty. Then the last crust of earth gave way, and cascaded into the nesting chamber, and glaring up out of the gloomy hole were two little ash-grey faces, with great dandelion-golden eyes. We all gave a whoop of triumph, and the owls blinked very rapidly and clicked their beaks like castanets. They looked so fluffy and adorable that I completely forgot all about owls' habits, and reached into the ruins of the nest-chamber and tried to pick one up. Immediately they transformed themselves from bewildered bundles consisting of soft plumage and great eyes, to swollen, belligerent furies. Puffing out the feathers on their backs, so that they looked twice their real size, they opened their wings on each side of their bodies like feathered shields, and, with clutching talons and snapping beaks, swooped at my hand. I sat back and sucked my bloodstained fingers.

"Have we got a thick cloth of some sort?" I asked – "something thicker than a handkerchief, with which to handle these innocent little dears?"

Dormouse sped off to the car and returned with an ancient and oil-stained towel. I doubled this over my hand and made a fresh attempt. This time I succeeded in grabbing one of the babies round the body, and although the towel kept off the attacks of his beak, I was still pricked by his clutching talons. Having got a good grip on the towel, he then refused to let go, and it took some time to disentangle his feet and pop him into a bag. His brother, now facing the enemy alone, seemed to lose a lot of his nerve, and he was much less trouble to catch and put in a bag. Hot, earth-stained, but feeling very pleased with ourselves, we re-entered the car. For the rest of the day we zig-zagged across the pampas, waiting for pairs of burrowing owls to fly out of the grass. Then we would wander about the spot until we had located the hole and proceed to dig it out. We met with more disappointments than successes, as Ian had predicted we would, but at the end of the day (having dug up what appeared to be several miles of tunnel), we returned to the *estancia* with a very satisfying bag of eight baby burrowing owls.

The Drunken Forest by Gerald Durrell

Passage 1

You have one hour to answer as many questions as you can. The questions are arranged in four sections, getting more difficult as they go on.

Section 1

Copy down the following sentences, supplying the missing words.

(a) The expedition was hunting for baby .... owls. (1)

(b) From the first hole they got .... owls, but by the end of the day they had caught .... (2)

(c) Two words that suggest this is not taking place in Britain are .... and .... (1)

(d) These words, in fact, suggest it is taking place in . . . Russia? Canada? U.S.A.? South America? (1)

(e) The expression that shows how the people felt *as they were digging* is .... (3)
The expression that shows how they felt *when they saw the young owls in the hole* is ....
The expression that tells us how they felt *at the end of the day* is ....

(f) Previously the towel (line 26) had been used to ....
Now, it was to be used to .... (2)

10

Section 2

1. Explain fully why the writer was "half-convinced that the burrow would prove empty." (line 12) 1
2. Explain why the second baby owl was "much less trouble to catch." (line 32) 1
3. "Clicked their beaks like castanets" What figure of speech is this? (line 16) 1
4. Complete this statement: *By using this figure of speech, the writer is trying to suggest the .... their beaks make, which is .... and ....* 3
5. Remembering to set it out correctly as *direct speech*, write down what Ian probably did say to them. (line 37) 2
6. Had they really dug "several miles of tunnel"? (line 38)
If not, what is the writer doing, and why has he done it? 2

10

Section 3

1. Why does the writer call the owls "innocent little dears" when they have just bitten him? (1)
2. Quote an expression from paragraph 2 which explains what had made the writer forget how savage little owls could be. (1)

3. Say which of these three statements is correct, *A*, *B* or *C*. (1)
   A – the young owls in the hole were female
   B – the young owls in the hole were male
   C – the young owls in the hole were of both sexes.
4. Quote the expression in the last paragraph that seems to prove you are right. (1)

5. | Compare, in detail, the structure of "little ash-grey faces" and "great dandelion-golden eyes". (line 14) (Look at Skills 9, 10, 13 and 14.) (3) |
   |---|

   See page 14 for worked example.
6. Explain how the *context* (the information given before and/or after), helps you to work out the meaning of the word "belligerent" (line 20). (2)
7. The behaviour of the owls soon reminded him about "owls' habits". Study lines 17–23, 29, what the owls did. Explain their actions in your own words, making it clear what actions you consider *defensive behaviour* and what was *offensive behaviour*. (4)

10

Section 4

1. Explain what the words in italics mean, paying particular attention to the various motions and movements involved. (4)
   "*probing* gently" (line 3)
   "earth *cascaded* into the nesting-chamber" (line 13)
   "*swooped* at my hand" (line 22)
   "we *zig-zagged* across the pampas" (line 34)
2. Using the information in the first paragraph, draw a diagram or diagrams to illustrate:
   (a) the shape and size of the burrow,
   (b) how the expedition divided it up to search it with "primitive reckoning".

   You may, if you wish, offer diagrams of the burrow from different angles. (6)
   You may label it if you wish.
   You may add *very brief* explanatory notes, provided they are made part of the illustration.

10

Dig Them Owls!

Passage 1, Section 3, Question 5

> Compare, in detail, the structure of "little ash-grey faces" and "great dandelion-golden eyes". (line 14) (3 marks)

Comment on requirements:
The key words here are "structure" and "detail". Only by going into detail will you gain full marks, and what you must look at in detail is the *structure*, i.e. how the phrases are put together, and what sort of words they are made from. Simply saying what the phrases mean will not answer the question.

Model answer:
The phrases are identical in structure: each consists of two adjectives describing a noun. The second adjective in each is made up of two words joined together. The adjectives in the first phrase describe the owls' faces, and contrast with the adjectives in the second which describe their eyes. "Great" and "small" contrast the size while "grey" and "golden" contrast the dull colour of the faces with the warm rich colour of the eyes. This contrast is increased by "ash" which suggests dead, dull things and "dandelion" which suggests something bright and alive.

Marker's comment:
The pupil has gained full marks. He has noted first that the two phrases are identical – adjective, compound adjective, noun. He has further noticed the contrast between the adjectives –

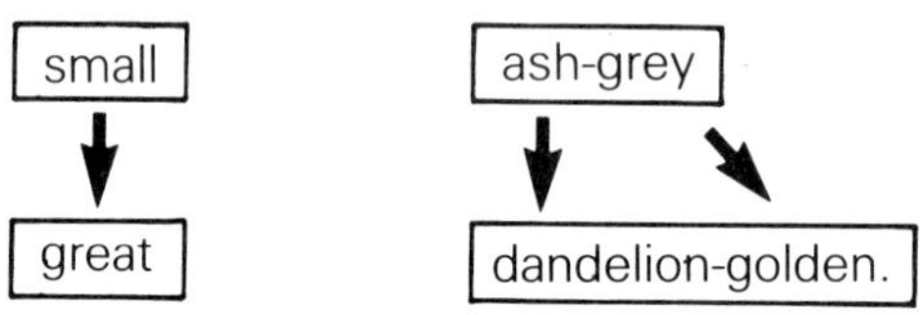

2 Home-Coming

The train rattled along the straight railway line which runs along the western edge of Romney Marsh from Ashford in Kent to the town of Rye.

From the window of a compartment in the front coach a red-headed girl stood watching for her first sight of the little town which had come to mean so much to her since her parents had gone abroad nearly three years ago. Not only was Penny Warrender coming home to the beloved Gay Dolphin – the hotel in Trader's Street kept by her aunt – but coming back with the certainty that within a week her father and mother would be home for six months at least. No wonder her heart banged with excitement. She always felt like this on the first day of the holidays, and although she was the sort of girl who made the best of every situation and did not really mind school, the summer holidays were something to be looked forward to all the year.

Penny was nearly sixteen, with clear, grey, wide-set eyes and a freckled nose rather nicely tip-tilted. Although quick-tempered and impetuous she had a way with her which made her many friends.

The train swung a little to the west and then, as she had expected, she saw Rye, a huddle of grey walls and red roofs clinging to its rocky hill, crowned by the church tower with the lazy summer sun glinting on its gilded weather vane.

And only a few hundred yards away from the church, down the cobbles of Trader's Street, was the dear old Dolphin. She wondered whether her aunt or cousin Jonathan would be at the station to meet her.

She leaned from the window and almost before she realised it, Aunt Margaret was helping her out with the luggage and giving her a hug of welcome.

"Let me look at you, Penny. You seem to be as untidy as usual and I'm sure you're hot and grubby. There's a fat air-mail letter from your father waiting for you at home. It *is* nice to see you again."

Penny felt tears spring to her eyes. Nobody could be kinder to her than Aunt Margaret who had always treated her as a daughter.

"I'm sorry I look untidy," she laughed. "It's just these loathsome school clothes. I believe they make us wear these ghastly garments just to humiliate us. I'll fling them off just as soon as I get in. May we walk home?"

"Of course. We'll leave the luggage and Vasson will pick it up in the car presently."

It was all just the same. Country people and holiday-makers waiting for buses in the station yard. The smell of hot tar. The hollyhocks standing like sentinels along the black fence. The crowds in Cinque Ports Street and an artist at the corner of every cobbled street. Penny and her aunt strolled in the sunshine up Lion Street to the church, and as Penny paused to look up at the great clock, the two Quarter Boys lifted their hammers and struck their bells as the hands pointed to a quarter to three.

"Are you busy, darling?" Penny said as they turned into Trader's Street. "Is the Dolphin full?"

"All I can manage, Penny. We're doing well, but don't worry, I haven't put anybody in your room . . . Aren't you going to ask about Jon?"

Penny felt herself going pink, but was too honest to pretend that she was not interested.

"He hasn't written for about six weeks. Has he broken up yet? Not that we can't manage without him, of course!"

"Of course we can, Penny. He's not been very good about writing to me this term either, but we must forgive him. I know he's been working very hard and he did admit once that his science master is pleased with him."

"Science!" Penny sighed. "Science is a closed book to me, and I hope it stays closed. I like learning things about real people . . . But when is he coming?"

"Tonight," Mrs Warrender smiled. "We'll have a little celebration dinner . . ."

Saucers Over the Moor by Malcolm Saville

Passage 2

You have 50 minutes to answer as many questions as you can. The questions are arranged in four sections, getting more difficult as they go on.

Section 1

1.	You are sending a letter to Penny during the holidays. Address an envelope to her using the information given in the passage.	(5)
2.	What does the abbreviation c/o stand for?	(1)
3.	How old was Penny when her parents left?	(1)
4.	Why do you think Penny's parents have gone abroad?	(1)
5.	Quote an expression that shows Penny was *popular*.	(1)
6.	Quote an expression that shows Penny was *adaptable*.	(1)
		10

Section 2

1. Why do you think Penny was in the *front* coach? (1)
2. Who do you think Vasson was? (1)
3. What colour was the weather vane? (1)
4. Penny felt herself 'going pink'. What feeling does this suggest? (1)
5. Why was she 'going pink' when Jon's name was mentioned? (1)
6. What relation was Jon to Penny? What relation was Jon to Aunt Margaret? (2)
7. Where was Jon at this particular time? (1)
8. What does the expression "broken up" (line 47) mean? (1)
9. Draw a simple clock face, marking the hours, 3, 6, 9, 12. On this, show what the time will be when the Quarter Boys *next* strike their bells. (1)

10

Section 3

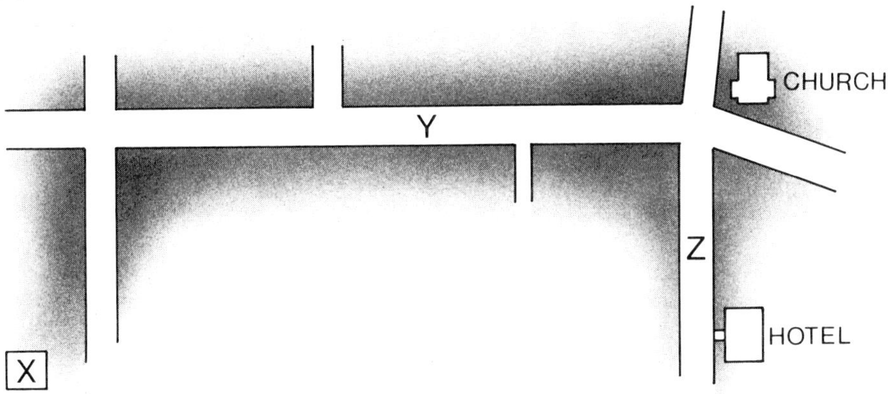

1. Study the street map above. What building would you find at (X), what is street Y called, what is street Z called? (3)
2. "hollyhocks standing like sentinels" (line 35)
   (a) What is a hollyhock?
   (b) What is a sentinel?
   (c) What figure of speech is this?
   (d) What does the writer think that hollyhocks and sentinels have in common? (4)
3. When Penny arrives, the little town is busy and bustling. She identifies three distinct groups of people – local country people, tourists, artists.
   What *distinctive* features of the town might attract these three separate groups? (3)

10

Section 4

1. Make clear the difference between "quick-tempered" and "impetuous". (line 14) (2)

2. Look at the sentence – "The smell of hot tar." (line 35)
What does it have in common with the two sentences that follow in terms of grammar?
Why has the writer chosen to write them this way?
(Look at skills 9, 13 and 14.) (2)

See below for worked example.

3. In your own words, write a sentence or two on each of the following, using the information given in the passage.
   Penny's attitude to school in general
   Penny's attitude to her school uniform
   Penny's attitude to science. (6)
4. Choose **two** features of Penny's *appearance* from the passage, and **two** things we are told about her *personality*. In your view, do these tally? (2)

10

Home-Coming

Passage 2, Section 4, Question 2.

Look at the sentence – "The smell of hot tar." (line 35)
What does it have in common with the two sentences that follow in terms of grammar?
Why has the writer chosen to write them this way? (2 marks)

Comment on requirements:
The key words here are 'in common . . . in terms of *grammar*' for the first mark: to say that the next two sentences also record details of the scene would not answer the question.

For the second mark, if the writer has *chosen* to write this way, it is to achieve some particular effect – so look for the effect.

Model answer:
"The smell of hot tar."
"The hollyhocks . . . . along the black fence."
"The crowds . . . every cobbled street."
What all of these have in common is that they are non-sentences – none of them has a verb. The writer has done this because it is the details themselves that are important (the smell, the hollyhocks, the crowds, the artist) and the writer wants to concentrate your attention on them, not him.

Marker's comment:
A straightforward two marks.

3 Come out, Come out, Whoever You Are.

He went into a bar and bought a glass of beer. He sat at a table near the door and stared at the street. A piano was being played in the public bar. Daytrippers sang 'Knees Up Mother Brown' and 'Knocked Them in the Old Kent Road'. At the table opposite his, two girls in the company of two foreign sailors drank pink gins and smoked cigarettes from tin drums.

Coover sipped his beer and thought, it all fits. It wasn't just the Morris; if it had only been that then he might have put it down to chance, a mad driver determined to run someone down for crazy, private reasons of his own. It was more than just the incident with the car. Ten days ago, at the office, he had received a telephone call from a man who would not give his name. The conversation had been simple and short.

'You remember me, don't you, Coover?'

'Who's speaking?'

'No names, no pack drill. You remember me well. I'll see that you don't get the chance to forget me.'

And then the telephone had gone dead in Coover's hand. What was the meaning of the conversation? More important, who had made the call? Coover thought about the voice: a hard, metallic voice, uncultured, London, probably the voice of a man in his middle thirties, although it wasn't possible to be sure. It was a joke, nothing more than a silly joke. Perhaps someone in the despatch department; there were always jokers in the packing room, men who relieved the tedium of endless balls of string, sealing wax and bales of brown wrapping paper with harmless antics like sewing up someone's pockets or sending a parcel of pebbles to someone's address.

That was it: nothing more than a harmless joke. Then, five days later, the anonymous letter arrived at Coover's home. Written on an incongruous piece of pink, scented note paper with broad white margins, the message said: *Remember me, Coover? I am going to bloody kill you. Watch for me.* It had been written in a childish hand, the letters looped together. It had been done with a ballpoint pen and was unsigned.

It all fits, Coover thought. The telephone call, the note, and now the black Morris. It was a ghastly syllogism.* Someone, perhaps passing in the crowds even now, at this moment, was going to kill him.

It was a senseless affair. Why should anyone want him dead? What harm had he ever done to anyone in his life? When he thought of his life, when he tried to consider it as a whole, he saw only an unbroken line stretching back to a point where all his memories seemed to stop. When he tried to take an aerial view, as it were, of his own existence, he saw a map etched in monochrome. He was an ordinary man. He did an ordinary job. He was not the material from which assassinations are made.

He finished his beer. A sudden gust of cold wind, dragging discarded cellophane and shards of seaside litter across the promenade, made him shiver. The two foreign sailors – were they Italian? French? – were making unambiguous signs to the girls they had picked up. A great deal of laughter, the chattering of the piano, the sound of shuffling feet, the raucous cries of the daytrippers – all this was going on around him, bombarding his senses, and yet he felt he was not a part of the same planet. And perhaps this was true: when someone is trying to murder you, all at once you are travelling in a different galaxy.

* *Syllogism* – an argument with two premises from which a conclusion is drawn, e.g. Birds can fly. A seagull is a bird. Therefore seagulls can fly.

Come out, Come out, Whoever You Are by Thomas McCann

Passage 3

You have one hour to answer as many questions as you can. The questions are arranged in four sections, getting more difficult as they go on.

Section 1

1. What children's game does the title remind you of? (1)
2. List the three events that made Coover think that someone was trying to kill him.
   1) Ten days ago ....
   2) Five days ago ....
   3) And today .... (3)
3. Quote a *phrase* that explains what at first Coover thought the phone call might be due to. (1)

4. He gives **two** examples of the sort of jokes his workmates might play. What are they? (1)
5. Quote the *word* that tells you why the men do such things. What does it mean? (2)
6. What sort of place did Coover work in? Give a reason for your answer. (2)

10

Section 2

1. Why did Coover feel that a threat to kill him was "a senseless affair"? (1)
2. Quote two expressions from the passage that give the meaning of 'anonymous'. (2)
3. What words (repeated in both letter and phone call) suggest the threats come from someone from Coover's past? (1)
4. In lines 18–19 the voice is described. Quote the words that tell you about (a) the dialect, and (b) the accent. (2)
5. What was "incongruous" about the letter? Explain your answer clearly. (line 26) (Look at Skills 3 and 8.) (2)

   See page 22 for worked example.
6. Coover notices that the handwriting is "in a childish hand" and written "with a ballpoint pen". If you asked him what he made of these two features, what he deduced, what might he answer? Give a separate answer for each feature. (2)
7. Explain why you think that "raucous cries" is better than 'loud cries', (line 45) and "shards of seaside litter" is better than 'bits of seaside litter'. (line 42) (2)

10

Section 3

1. "No names, no pack drill." (line 14)
   (a) This is an example of what language feature?
   (b) Where probably did this expression originate?
   (c) Explain what it means. (3)
2. You will have noted that this writer is very *exact* in the *details* he gives, hoping to make you, in turn, draw very exact and detailed conclusions. Look at the following details – why do you think each one was so exactly included?
   1) making the daytrippers sing *Knees Up Mother Brown*
   2) having the girls drink *pink gins*
   3) asking . . . were they *Italian? French?* (3)
3. Do the expressions in the last paragraph, "not a part of the same planet" and "in a different galaxy" mean the same thing or is there a difference? Has the writer done this for any reason? (2)
4. What comments would you want to make on the writer's choice of name – Coover? (2)

10

Section 4

1. In the second last paragraph, Coover has two different images, pictures in his mind, of how his life looks. What are they? What does each picture tell you *about* his life? (4)
2. "ghastly syllogism" (line 32) – Do you think it is a syllogism? See footnote. Give a reason for your answer.
   Why obviously does Coover think it's a syllogism? (2)
3. The first and last paragraphs are dominated by the noisy daytrippers and the two girls and foreign sailors. In between, comes Coover's realisation that somebody is trying to kill him. Give two reasons why the writer wanted to construct the passage this way, and what advantages he might gain from so doing. (4)

10

Come out, Come out, Whoever You Are.

Passage 3, Section 2, Question 5.

What was "incongruous" about the letter?
Explain your answer clearly. (line 26) (2 marks)

Comment on requirements:
An easy question if you know what "incongruous" means – but note that you will still have to explain it clearly, which means using your own words. If you don't know what "incongruous" means, look at the passage. The context (that part of the passage where the word appears) should help you to work out what "incongruous" means.

Model answer:
You don't expect a death threat to be written on pink, scented note-paper, something that would be more suited to a love letter.

Marker's comment:
The pupil has picked out two pieces of information – the fact that the letter is a death threat, and the fact that it is on pink, scented paper – and in collating them, has noted that the kind of paper used does not go together with what it is used for. From this he has deduced that "incongruous" describes an unsuitable combination, two things that you would not expect to find together, or an unexpected combination of things.

4 A Mere Morsel

When we were children our father often worked on the night-shift. Once it was spring-time, and he used to arrive home, black and tired, just as we were downstairs in our nightdresses. Then night met morning face to face, and the contact was not always happy. Perhaps it was painful to my father to see us gaily entering upon the day into which he dragged himself soiled and weary. He didn't like going to bed in the spring morning sunshine.

But sometimes he was happy, because of his long walk through the dewy fields in the first daybreak. He loved the open morning, the crystal and the space, after a night down pit. He watched every bird, every stir in the trembling grass, answered the whinnying of the peewits, and tweeted to the wrens. If he could, he also would have whinnied and tweeted and whistled in a native language that wasn't human. He liked non-human things best.

One sunny morning we were all sitting at table when we heard his heavy slurring walk up the entry. We became uneasy. His was always a disturbing presence, trammelling. He passed the window darkly, and we heard him go into the scullery and put down his tin bottle. But directly he came into the kitchen we felt at once that he had something to communicate. No one spoke. We watched his black face for a second.

"Give me a drink," he said.

My mother hastily poured out his tea. He went to pour it out into his saucer. But instead of drinking it he suddenly put something on the table among the tea-cups. A tiny brown rabbit! A small rabbit, a mere morsel, sitting against the bread as still as if it were a made thing.

"Where did you get it, Father?"

"I picked it up," he said, wiping his fore-arm over his mouth and beard.

"Where?"

"It's a wild one!" came my mother's quick voice.

"Yes, it is."

"Then why did you bring it?" cried my mother.

"It would die," we shouted.

"Yes, and it will die now. And then there'll be another outcry."

My mother set her face against the tragedy of dead pets. Our hearts sank.

"It won't die, Father, will it? Why will it? It won't."

"I s'd think not," said my father.

"You know well enough it will. Haven't we had it all before!" said my mother.

"They dunna always pine," replied my father testily.

But my mother reminded him of other little wild animals he had brought, which had sulked and refused to live, and brought storms of tears and trouble in our house of lunatics. Trouble fell on us. The little rabbit sat on our lap, unmoving, its eyes wide and dark. We brought it milk, warm milk, and held it to its nose. It sat as still as if it was far away, retreated down some deep burrow, hidden, oblivious. We wetted its mouth and whiskers with drops of milk. It gave no sign, did not even shake off the wet, white drops. Somebody began to shed a few secret tears.

Adolf by D. H. Lawrence

Passage 4

You have one hour to answer as many questions as you can. The questions are arranged in four sections, getting more difficult as they go on.

Section 1

1. What was Lawrence's father's occupation? (1)
2. Why would he have carried a "tin bottle"? (1)
3. Give another word for "scullery". (1)
4. There is a contrast in the sentence, "Perhaps it was painful . . ." (line 4) Quote the contrasting words or phrases. By examining these, explain fully who or what are being contrasted. (3)
5. From the information given in paragraph 2, outline *in your own words* how the father felt towards Nature. (3)
6. Suggest a reason why he felt this way. (1)

10

Section 2

1. Quote the first words the father says. From this, what would you suggest about his relationship with his wife? (2)
2. Explain clearly why the mother objects to the children keeping the rabbit. (2)
3. What is unusual about the sentence, "A tiny brown rabbit!"? What effect is the writer trying to create by doing this? (2)
4. "A small rabbit . . sitting . . . as if it were a made thing." (lines 22–23)
   (a) What figure of speech is this?
   (b) What does the expression "a made thing" mean here?

(c) Why do the children think the rabbit is like this? (3)

5. Look carefully at the words "uneasy", "disturbing" and "trammelling" in paragraph 3. Show how each word, in turn, contributes to your understanding of how the children felt on their father's return.
(Look at Skills 3, 5, 8, 10 and 11.) (3)

See page 26 for worked example.

6. "a mere morsel" (line 22) – what effect does the word *mere* have on our response to the idea of *morsel*? (1)

10

Section 3

1. In paragraph 3 'slurring' is a very unusual word to describe someone walking, being usually used to describe .... But what the writer cleverly suggests here is ....
Rewrite this, supplying the necessary ideas to complete it. (2)
2. Construct a similar answer for the word "whinnying", (line 10). (2)
3. During the course of their conversation, tension mounts between the mother and father. Indicate **two** ways in which tension is increased, explaining in each case how this shows an increase in the tension. (4)
4. Explain, in your own words, what is meant by the expression "the crystal and the space". (line 8) (2)

10

Section 4

1. "Night met morning face to face." (line 3). The writer wants us to see night as representing the father and morning as representing the children.
   (a) What two ideas might "night" suggest about Lawrence's attitude to his father?
   (b) What two ideas might "morning" suggest about Lawrence's attitude to the children? (4)
2. Lawrence also says, (line 15), that his father passed the window *darkly. Darkly* suggests a number of things both about (a) the father himself, and (b) the children's attitude to him.
   Try to explain **one** thing it suggests to you about (a) and **one** thing it suggests about (b). (2)
3. Do you think that the image of the rabbit hidden "down some deep burrow" is a very good one at this particular point of the story? Give a clear explanation of your decision. (2)
4. This passage has several examples of the very short sentence being used to good effect.
   Quote two examples and explain why each is particularly effective coming where it does (i.e. in its *context*). (2)

10

A Mere Morsel

Passage 4, Section 2, Question 5.

> Look carefully at the words "uneasy", "disturbing" and "trammelling" in paragraph 3. Show how each word, in turn, contributes to your understanding of how the children felt on their father's return. (3 marks)

Comment on requirements:
Two common words and an uncommon one; but they all describe how the children *felt*: so it is important to get a clear idea of how they felt overall, before looking at the contribution of each word.

Model answer:
The children feel tense and on edge when their father appears, as they expected something to happen. "Uneasy" suggests the beginning of this feeling – they have been calm and relaxed up to now. "Disturbing" carries on the idea of the father upsetting the peace of the house, casting a dark shadow in the sunny morning. "Trammelling" suggests that they didn't feel as free and easy once he was around.

Marker's comment:
A good, methodical and sensible answer – the pupil has first of all stated in his *own* words how the children feel, and then gone on to look at each word in turn, explaining how it contributes to the overall effect. The pupil's success here stems from the fact that he has looked closely at the context, and pictured the situation vividly. The gloss of the difficult word "trammelling" develops nicely from the gloss of the two easier words, and all are taken from the reader's own picture of how the children *must* have felt in those circumstances.

5 An African Looks at the English

Every young African travelling to England from the colonies looks forward to the England he has been told about. I too looked forward to my first visit to London. At home, I was used to Africans working as porters and sweepers while Europeans made us believe they always worked as skilled technicians, executives, supervisors, and in the professions. We had been brought up to know that European houses were modern and clean and that their wives were 'Memsahibs', never cooking, sweeping floors, or polishing furniture. Every European seemed to own a car – sometimes two. Of course, as a young politician, I learned the destiny of my country was in the hands of the English people and I imagined all of them would know where Kenya was.

On arrival at London airport, I was struck by the fact that Englishmen worked as porters and sweepers and waiters. Some of them spoke bad English which I could not understand. Later when I lived in Oxford, I met students and many other people and began to see them as human beings. I visited homes of friends and saw wives and mothers look after their homes and children like any simple mother among my people. I met Members of Parliament who walked to work and labourers in the streets. I visited coal-mining areas and met humble workers to whom colour was a curiosity, but not a scale of values.

One of my biggest disappointments was the sight of London. Drab, black and grey ugly buildings – cold and big with no laughter or gaiety. This was not the London settlers had boasted so much about. Contrasted with my first impressions of New York later, I found the English very cold and reserved and although one saw thousands of people in the street one still felt all alone.

My second disappointment was the ignorance of the majority of Englishmen about the conditions and peoples of the colonies. On several occasions at the House of Commons, I met M.P.s whose ignorance of Kenya and East Africa was similar to that of the coal miners I visited in various parts of Britain! And yet in their hands lay the destiny of millions of people. Since those days in 1955, I have been struck by the increased awareness of Africa and the outside world.

On first impression, I was convinced that there was no colour bar in Britain, but this is not true and you see this the longer you live in London. Students looking for accommodation tell stories of telephone calls made to landladies and promises made, but when the student turns up, the landlady says it was a mistake – there had been no vacant rooms at all!

At Oxford, I found life stimulating and challenging. I enjoyed my time there in discussions and debates with fellow students and the lecturers and professors. Here I felt that there was the equality denied my people in Kenya and the freedom to air one's views. In fact, life at Oxford was such that I was able to develop my ideas on the future of Kenya by writing a booklet – *The Kenya Question: An African Answer* – and many articles. This part of my life was my greatest experience. Even today when I think of England, my student days at Ruskin remain my most cherished memory.

By Tom Mboya, then General Secretary of Kenya National Union, from *The Sunday Times Colour Magazine.*

Passage 5

Section 1

1. Why did the author look forward to his first visit to London? (1)
2. On arriving in England, did the author go to Oxford at once? How do you know? (1)
3. Which of the following could Mboya claim to be?
   – Member of Parliament
   – politician
   – Kenyan
   – colonialist
   – East African
   – student (2)
4. Explain why the writer was "struck by the fact that Englishmen worked as porters and sweepers and waiters". (line 12) (1)
5. Which did he actually visit first, London or New York? How do you know? (2)
6. What part of his stay in England did the writer remember with most pleasure? Quote the *phrase* that tells you this. (2)
7. What is "Ruskin" (line 41)? (1)

10

Section 2

1. In your own words, explain fully what disappointed the writer about London. (2)
2. Explain clearly how he felt London differed from New York. (2)
3. What is meant by "the colonies" (line 1)? Quote a phrase from later in the paragraph that expresses this idea. (2)
4. ". . . *made us believe* they *always* worked . . ." (line 4)
   What do the words in italics tell us about the accounts that Europeans gave of their lives 'back home'?
   Quote a single word from later in the same paragraph that continues the idea. (2)
5. Explain why the landladies made promises to students only to withdraw them when the students appeared. (2)

10

Section 3

1. (a) Until the writer moved to Oxford, how did he regard the English?
   (b) How did his feelings change?
   (c) Why did they change? (3)
2. In your own words, say how the writer found life at Oxford. (2)
3. What 'equality' did he find there that was lacking in Kenya? (line 37) (1)
4. In your own words, explain what changes the writer has noticed in Britain since he first visited here. Can you suggest any reason why such changes might have occurred? (2)
5. By examining the immediate context work out what "Memsahibs" were. (line 6)

Section 4

1. Explain the use made of the exclamation mark in lines 27 and 34. (Look at Skills 13 and 14.) (2)

   See page 30 for worked example.
2. Explain the use made of the dash in lines 8, 20 and 33.
3. Choose **one** of the following pairs of words – "stimulating and challenging" (line 35) **or** "discussions and debates". (line 36.) Make clear what you understand the distinction between the two words to be.
4. ". . colour was a curiosity, but not a scale of values." (line 18) Explain clearly what the writer is saying here about the workers' attitudes.
5. "Some of them spoke bad English . . ." (line 12)
   Explain two ways in which the writer might have found the English of the workers to be 'bad'. (2)
6. "An African Looks at the English"
   In what ways does the choice of words in the title reflect the sort of ignorance discussed by the writer in the passage? (2)

10

An African Looks at the English

Passage 5, Section 4, Question 1.

Explain the use made of the exclamation mark in lines 27 and 34.(2 marks)

Comment on requirements:
An exclamation mark indicates a definite tone of voice – the question here is really why has the writer chosen to make the sentences in question exclamations, rather than simply statements. What is he exclaiming about? Two marks suggest two reasons, one for each case.

Model answer:
In the first case the exclamation mark expresses the author's surprise and amazement that the M.P.s knew no more about Africa than ordinary people – he had expected them to know better.

In the second case it expresses his disbelief – of the landlady's claim that there really hadn't been a room available after all. It is as if he is saying to the reader, 'Would you believe it?'

Marker's comment:
A good careful answer. People usually exclaim when they are surprised by something, but it is important to say *what it is* that is surprising in each case. The exclamation mark invites the reader to share the author's surprise. The pupil has used a good technique in answering the second part of the question – he has explained the exclamation mark by using another expression which has the same effect.

6 Brotherly Alarm

There were no curtains up. The window was a hard edged block the colour of the night sky. Inside the bedroom the darkness was of a gritty texture. The wardrobe and bed were blurred shapes in the darkness. Silence.

Billy moved over, towards the outside of the bed. Jud moved with him, leaving one half of the bed empty. He snorted and rubbed his nose. Billy whimpered. They settled. Wind whipped the window and swept along the wall outside.

Billy turned over. Jud followed him and cough-coughed into his neck. Billy pulled the blankets up round his ears and wiped his neck with them. Most of the bed was now empty, and the unoccupied space quickly cooled. Silence. Then the alarm rang. The noise brought Billy upright, feeling for it in the darkness, eyes shut tight. Jud groaned and hutched back across the cold sheet. He reached down the side of the bed and knocked the clock over, grabbed for it, and knocked it further away.

"Come here, you bloody thing."

He stretched down and grabbed it with both hands. The glass lay curved in one palm, while the fingers of his other hand fumbled amongst the knobs and levers at the back. He found the lever and the noise stopped. Then he coiled back into bed and left the clock lying on its back.

"The bloody thing."

He stayed in his own half of the bed, groaning and turning over every few minutes. Billy lay with his back to him, listening. Then he turned his cheek slightly from the pillow.

"Jud?"

"What?"

"Tha'd better get up."

No answer.

"Alarm's gone off tha knows."

"Think I don't know?"

He pulled the blankets tighter and drilled his head into the pillow. They both lay still.

"Jud?"

"What?"

"Tha'll be late."

"O, shut it."

"Clock's not fast tha knows."

"I said **shut it**."

He swung his fist under the blankets and thumped Billy in the kidneys.

"Gi'o'er! That hurts!"

"Well shut it then."

"I'll tell my mam on thi."

Jud swung again. Billy scuffled away into the cold at the edge of the bed, sobbing. Jud got out, sat on the edge of the bed for a moment, then stood up and felt his way across the room to the light switch. Billy worked his way back to the centre and disappeared under the blankets.

"Set t'alarm for me, Jud. For seven.'

"Set it thi sen."

"Go on, thar up."

Jud parted Billy's sweater and shirt, and used the sweater for a vest. Billy snuggled down in Jud's place, making the springs creak. Jud looked at the humped blankets, then walked across and pulled them back, stripping the bed completely.

A Kestrel for a Knave by Barry Hines

Passage 6

You have one hour to answer as many questions as you can. The questions are arranged in four sections, getting more difficult as they go on.

Section 1

1. The opening sentence is a short statement of fact.
   (a) Why does the writer choose to begin this way?
   (b) What does this tell us about the family's circumstances?
   (c) Quote two other pieces of information from the passage that support your answer to (b). (4)
2. What impression do you form of the relationship between Billy and Jud *before anyone speaks*. Give at least two reasons in support. (3)
3. What does the first piece of dialogue tell you about how Jud feels when the alarm goes off? Give a reason for your answer. (2)

4. Why does the writer say "cough-coughed" (line 7) rather than just 'coughed'? (1)

10

Section 2

1. Justify the question mark after "Jud?" when Billy first speaks. (line 23) (1)
2. What is unusual about the sentence "No answer."? Why is it written this way? (2)
3. Why is **shut it** printed in heavy type in line 36 but not in line 34? (1)
4. Billy lay "listening". (line 21) What was he listening for? (1)
5. Why does Jud pull back all the blankets from the bed? (1)
6. Look carefully at the first three paragraphs.
   (a) Choose from them a word that relates to our sense of sight, one of sound, one of touch.
   (b) On which of the three senses does the writer seem to be concentrating in these paragraphs?
   (c) Suggest two reasons for this concentration. (4)

10

Section 3

1. What effect is the writer trying to create by placing the word "Silence" in a sentence by itself, and repeating this in paragraph 3? (1)
2. Look carefully at the conversation between Jud and Billy. Write down one thing you learn from this about (a) Jud, (b) Billy, and (c) the relationship between them. (3)
3. "Wind whipped the window and swept along the wall outside."
   (a) What is this device called?
   (b) What effect is the writer trying to create by using it here? (2)
4. Explain why "drilled" (line 29) is an unusual word to use here but why it is nevertheless a good way to describe Jud's movement. (2)
5. What is surprising about the expression "darkness was of a gritty texture"? What do you think the writer means by this? (2)

10

Section 4

1.

> Whimpering and sobbing are two kinds of crying – but different!
> Use the context of the words (what is happening in the story at each point) to bring out the difference in meaning between "whimper" and "sob". (line 5 and line 42)
> (Look at Skills 1, 3, 10 and 12.) (4)

See page 34 for worked example.

2. Quote four examples of non-Standard English from the passage. In what ways does the use of such language help to create and define the characters? (4)
3. "Hutched" (line 11) is a very unusual verb. We know the noun as in

rabbit-*hutch*. A "hutch" is, according to the dictionary, a small, cramped house. The poet Milton used it as a verb, meaning to 'hoard'. Is it connected here with "hitched"?

Try to describe as clearly as you can what action the writer is describing here in using this word. (2)

4. In paragraph four, (lines 15–18), Jud's actions are listed in a sequence of verbs.

   Choose the two from this paragraph that you find most effective, giving a reason for your choice. (2)

5. "Jud parted Billy's sweater and shirt, and used the sweater for a vest." (line 48) What does the word "parted" mean here? What does this action tell us about Jud's character? (2)

   10

Brotherly Alarm

Passage 6, Section 4, Question 1.

Whimpering and sobbing are two kinds of crying – but different! Use the context of the words (what is happening in the story at each point) to bring out the difference in meaning between "whimper" and "sob". (line 5 and line 42) (4 marks)

Comment on requirements:
There is a lot of free information in this question, so use it. You are told that there *is* a difference between whimpering and sobbing, and you are told how to find it – by looking at different contexts. Again it is a question of using your imagination to picture the scene clearly. (Cf. Passage 4, Section 2, Question 5.) Four marks suggests a detailed explanation in each case.

Model answer:
In the first case, Billy whimpers because he is trying to get away from Jud into his own area of the bed, but Jud keeps following him and won't allow him any space. Every time Billy moves to get space, Jud moves too and takes it away. His whimper is a kind of cry of frustration and defeat. In the second case, Jud has hit Billy and actually hurt him, as sobbing is a cry of pain, a stronger sort of crying than whimpering, which is weak and feeble.

Marker's comment:
The pupil has used the context well, especially in the first case, where it is less easy to work out what Billy is crying about.

The pupil does well to deal with each word separately before bringing them together at the end.

7 Kronk

A coarse voice, shouting with unholy glee, rang across the shingly beach. Kronk came barging across the sand, brandishing his heavy whip in triumph.

"Ach, Herr Captain," he gloated, pulling up breathless on the shore. "You have caught that accursed English flyer! And Kronk gets his 20,000 marks, hein? Ach!" He spat in Barry's direction, "I knew he was a fraud the minute I set eyes on him. Yes, my fine Herr Falconer, I knew you were a spy all the time. And now I'm going to flog you till your ribs show!"

Captain Müller stepped forward, confronting Kronk abruptly.

"If you knew all the time the prisoner was a spy," he demanded sternly, "why did you not at once inform the Reich? So far from receiving 20,000 marks, you are liable to severe penalties for your flagrant neglect of duty!"

This was certainly a poser, but Kronk, in his present cock-a-hoop mood, was equal to any occasion.

"Because he held me prisoner, Herr Captain," he almost blubbered, squeezing out crocodile tears. "Kept me locked up in a cellar, he did – kicked me – tortured me! Ach, he beat me black and blue only last week with this very whip. Jawohl, he, a cursed Englander, struck me – a servant of the Fuehrer!"

The sheer magic of the Fuehrer's name! The mere mention transformed Captain Müller as if a mask had dropped from his face. Barry saw with a start that the man's calm, stolid features were calm and stolid no longer. His thick lips were drawn back in a snarl. His pale eyes glinted with a cold blue glare – the light of fanatical cruelty.

"You – struck – a – servant – of – the – Fuehrer!" he whispered, focusing his gaze on Barry Falconer, with an almost animal-like stare.

But the expression was only a fleeting one. As Müller turned once more to Kronk, he was his old calm, matter-of-fact self again.

"Very well!" he said curtly, his face once more a mask. "You may give him thirty lashes – no more!"

Hemmed about by his foes, their faces agrin with relish, Barry was propelled towards a cliff, and thrust roughly, with his back against the rock. The clean-shaven young Englishman's wrists were throbbing hotly; his arms were aching excruciatingly from the cramped and brutal fashion in which they were tied. He suspected also that his recent rough handling had reopened the gash in his shoulder, which was once more giving him gip. But as he stood at bay against the crag, his eyes flickered whimsically on Kronk, who, licking his lips evilly, came sliding cat-like towards him, the sinuous lash flicking the sand like the swishing tail of some purring tiger.

"Don't be afraid, Kronk!" he jeered. "I can't get at you!"

Swish! The pitiless slashing thong, with all the brute strength of Kronk's powerful arm behind it, snaked with sickening deliberate force around the Sea Falcon's injured shoulder. The fiery biting agony nearly turned the young Englishman faint. His face blenched visibly beneath its tan and his teeth clamped down angrily upon his lower lip, but he neither flinched nor cried out. Grinning like a demon, Kronk whirled up his arm for another and even more vicious stroke, aimed straight at the Sea Falcon's wound, when:

"Hi, you skunk! Drop that whip!"

Shouting the words, a savage figure came charging down the cliff, a tousled, dishevelled figure in a shrunken blue R.A.F. tunic. Griff – but a Griff possessed! Hurling himself with catapult force on the startled Emil Kronk, he tore the whip from the torturer's grasp, and flung it on the sand. Like a piston-rod, his fist shot out in a savage, driving blow that crunched straight into Kronk's unshaven jaw, and sent the bully, with an animal-like howl, sprawling upon the beach.

"Now you beauties, stand back. Or – by Harry – I'll blow you all to Berlin!"

The Sea Falcon by Erroll Collins

Passage 7

Section 1

1. Where would you normally expect to find this sort of writing? (1)
2. Look carefully at the first part of the passage – to "Jawohl, he, a cursed Englander, struck me . . ."
   What sort of person *is* Kronk?
   Select, for your answer, **four** details or expressions which are intended to influence strongly what you think of Kronk. Comment on the intended effect of each one. (4)
3. What sort of person is Müller *in this part of the passage*? (1)
4. What makes him change later on? (1)
5. What sort of person is he seen to be later on? (1)
6. How does the writer convey these new qualities? (2)

10

Section 2

1. (a) Kronk and Müller belong to the same nation. Which nation?
   (b) Give two reasons for your conclusion.
   (c) What does the writer intend you to think of this nation? Make at least two clear points. (4)
2. Read carefully the description of Kronk lashing Falconer. (lines 39–45) Study carefully the contrasts between Falconer's behaviour *in these lines* and Kronk's behaviour *in the passage*. Choose **three** details that seem to you to pinpoint the differences between the two nations involved. (3)
3. Using the evidence of the passage and the picture, what was Falconer's job in the Armed Forces? What service was he in? (1)
4. Look at the last line of the passage. What is Griff doing, do you think, as he says this? (1)

9

Section 3

1. Does the picture suit the *style* of the passage? Give **two** reasons for your answer. (2)
2. Explain what these rather slangy and colloquial expressions mean – "a poser" (line 12), "giving him gip" (line 34). (2)
3. Explain clearly the three *different* uses made of the hyphen (dash) by the writer in these expressions – "cock-a-hoop" (line 12), "struck me – a servant of the Fuehrer . ." (line 17), "You – struck – a – servant – of – the – Fuehrer!" (line 23) (3)
4. Identify the language feature or figurative device in the following – "the pitiless slashing thong . ." (line 39), "like a piston-rod, his fist shot out . ." (line 50), "crocodile tears" (line 15) (3)

10

Section 4

1. Explain how its context helps you to understand the meaning of the word "sinuous". (line 39) (2)
2. Choose from the passage **two** expressions that seem to you hackneyed clichés.
   (Look at Skills 1, 12 and 13.) (2)
3. Choose **two** of the characters – Kronk, Müller, Griff, Falconer – and explain clearly in what ways these characters seem to you to be rather 'clichéd' as well.
   You may, if you wish, explain why you find quite the reverse to be true, that the characters are imaginative and convincing, realistic. (4)
4. Choose **one** of the four characters and discuss to what extent:
   (a) how that character behaves,
   (b) how the character talks,
   (c) how the character looks in appearance
   all help to reinforce and complement one another.
   (Do *not* use the evidence of the picture in this answer.) (3)

5. By studying the behaviour of the main characters in the passage, chart the development of the 'Sea Falcon's' predicament, as it unfolds in the passage, detailing each separate stage. (4)

15

See below for worked example.

Kronk

Passage 7, Section 4, Question 5.

By studying the behaviour of the main characters in the passage, chart the development of the 'Sea Falcon's' predicament, as it unfolds in the passage, detailing each separate stage.

(4 marks)

Comment on requirements:
This question requires you to study the overall structure of the passage, and to identify the sections it is made up of. It is likely that paragraphing will be a useful guide here, coupled with the hero's changes of fortune. It will also be necessary to distinguish main characters from secondary ones.

Model answer:
The passage starts with the 'Sea Falcon' being threatened by Kronk, but then Müller steps in and prevents Kronk from carrying out his threat. Then Kronk changes Müller's mind by saying that Falconer "struck a servant of the Fuehrer" and Müller gives Kronk permission to whip him. The Sea Falcon defies his enemies and jeers at Kronk but the punishment begins. Then Griff intervenes and our hero is saved.

Marker's comment:
The pupil has answered the question by giving a brief summary of each stage, but the important thing is that he concentrates on the relevant details – the crucial changes of attitude that take place between Müller, Kronk and Falconer.

8 What Do People Need to Eat?

Fig. 10. Comparison of the Daily Intake of Calories by Regions.*

Region	*Calorie Supplies*	*Calorie Requirements*
Far East	2,070	2,300
Africa	2,360	2,400
Latin America	2,470	2,400
Europe	3,040	2,600
North America	3,120	2,600
Oceania	3,250	2,600

* *Third World Food Survey*, F.A.O., 1963.

Note: The calorie requirement represents the average need in calories of a healthy person – based on the F.A.O. international requirement scale. In using these comparisons, allowance must be made for differing needs, e.g. a teenage athlete or a nursing mother in Europe may require at least 4,000 calories per day whilst an elderly, sedentary worker might well exist on a little over half of this intake. Moreover, climate and geographical location play a significant part in determining calorie requirements.

These comparisons indicate that the technologically advanced nations of Europe, North America and Oceania average about a twenty per cent excess of calorie requirements, Latin America and Africa generally satisfy the required level but the Far East calorie requirement is deficient by about 11 per cent, sometimes stretched over the whole year or emphasised in the pre-harvest void. Even in Latin America and Africa, with an apparently satisfactory level, there are areas of malnutrition and hunger resulting from the maldistribution of supplies or climatic irregularities in areas where stocks of food are insufficient, or non-existent, to bridge a lean year.

The calorie requirement level should be compared with Fig. 11 detailing the regional shares of the world's agricultural production. It is evident that the Far East, the area with the greatest deficiency, has, relative to population, a meagre proportion of the world's agricultural production.

A balanced diet requires various kinds of food in which two main energy suppliers are important. The *carbohydrates* – starch and sugars, etc. – are found in bread, milk, cereals, peas, beans, cakes, jam . . . and *fatty foods* include butter, cheese, bacon and peanuts. The body builders are the *proteins* found in meat, fish and eggs. To complete the balance certain vitamins, mineral salts and water are necessary. Most balanced diets ensure that the carbohydrates play a major role, provided the fat and protein levels are adequate. Fig. 12, however, illustrates the unbalanced nature of diets in various regions of the world.

Thus the North American eats about six times as much top-quality food as the peasant of the Far East. Represented diagrammatically, the difference is shown in Fig. 13.

Most countries rely on the basic cereals and starchy foods, supplemented and increasingly replaced in richer nations by a greater proportion of proteins and other protective foods. Figs. 12 and 13 illustrate that diets in the Far East are badly

balanced and, for the most part, minimal only. Diets in the Near East and Africa show a little less dependence on carbohydrates but the proportion is still too high. The alarming trend is that, whereas other regions are improving or maintaining a satisfactory calorie and protein intake, the Far East has regressed in the post-war period owing, no doubt, to the increased pressure of population. Fig. 14 illustrates this problem.

Except in the Far East the calorie intakes are reasonably adequate in the worst cases but the deficiency in proteins, especially of animal origin, is much more serious and in Africa, Latin America and the Far East the protein intake is much lower than that for developed regions. Animal protein level in North America is 66 grammes per day compared with 8 grammes in the Far East.

It is a sad comment on our times that the new American 'non-food' (a concoction of cellulose) should have been hailed as a 'miraculous scientific discovery'. It has plenty of bulk and no nutritional value whatsoever but prevents the stomach from feeling neglected. This is the scientists' answer to the diseases of the rich: an attempt to *reduce* animal protein intake and still allow the psychological satisfaction of mechanical eating.

Fig. 11. Regional Percentage Shares of the World's Agricultural Production and Population.*

Region	*Agricultural Production %*	*Population %*
Western Europe	15	11
E. Europe (incl. U.S.S.R.)	17	10
North America	21	7
Latin America	8	7
Far East	28	53
Near East	4	4
Africa	4	7
Oceania	3	1

* United Nations, Basic Study No. 7.

Fig. 12. Average Daily Calorie Intake Per Head of Population from Carbohydrates, Fats and Other Foods.

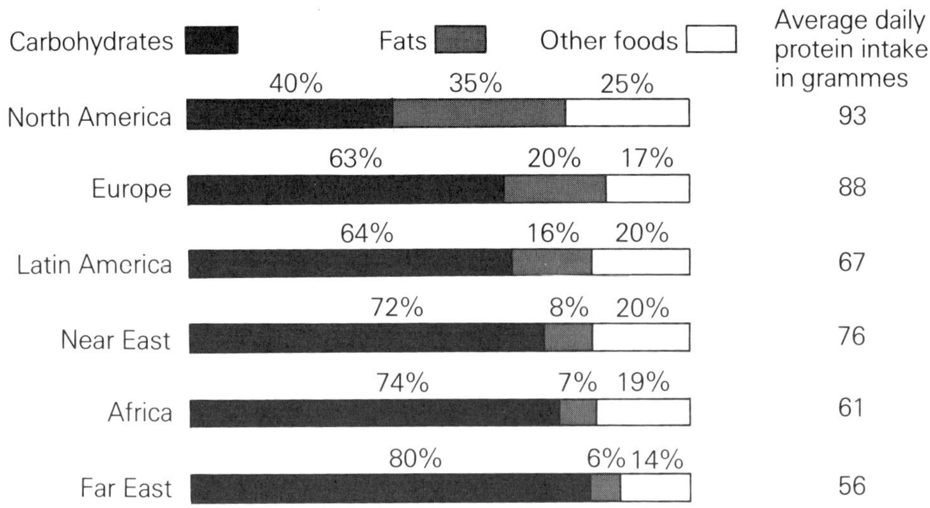

Fig. 13. Comparison of American and Indian Daily Diets.

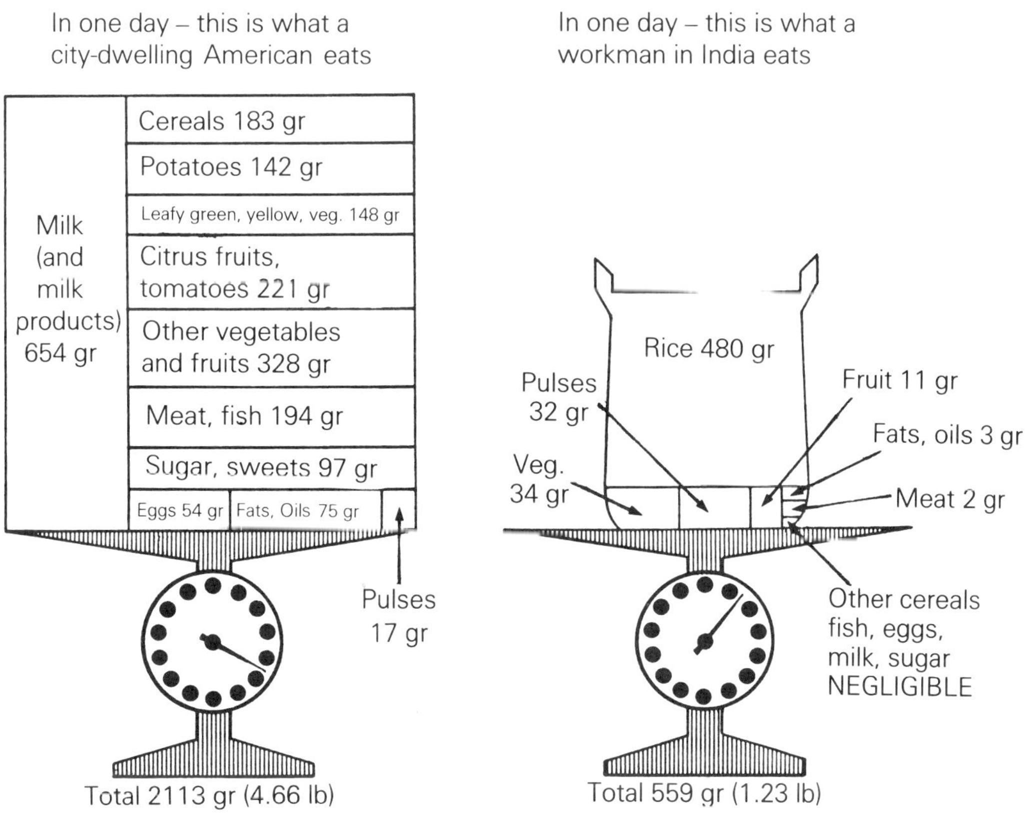

Source: *FAO.* Source: *USDA*

Fig. 14. Daily Calorie and Protein Intake by Regions.*

Region	*Calories*		*Total Proteins (grammes)*	
	Pre-war	*Recent*	*Pre-war*	*Recent*
Far East	2,120	2,070	63	56
Africa	2,180	2,360	61	61
Latin America	2,140	2,470	66	67
Europe	2,850	3,040	85	88
North America	3,140	3,120	89	93

* *Source*: Sukhatme, P. W. *The World's Hunger and Future Needs in Food Supplies: Journal of the Royal Statistical Society*. Series A. (General.) Vol. 124

Passage 8

Section 1

(Based on Fig. 10 and relevant commentary)

1. Give a reason to justify your conclusion that this extract is taken from a book. (1)
2. What *is* a calorie? (1)
3. Why should a teenage athlete require so many calories? (2)
4. Why should a nursing mother require so many calories? (1)
5. Why should an elderly sedentary worker need a much smaller intake? (2)
6. *In general terms*, what does the writer (in Fig. 10) have to say about the calorie intake in Oceania?
   Where *is* Oceania? (2)
7. Explain clearly why the required *average* intake of calories is lower in the Far East than in North America. (2)

11

Section 2

(Based on Figs. 10 & 11 and relevant commentary)

1. Copy down this table of common foods. Beside each write whether that food is a carbohydrate, fat, protein or other food.

Eggs	
Bread	
Jam	
Butter	
Water	
Sugar	

(3)

2. Latin America and Africa are both near the required calorie intake – yet there are problems. *In your own words*, explain what the problems are in these areas. (3)
3. What are the main functions, in terms of healthy development, of (a) proteins and (b) carbohydrates? (2)
4. Explain what you see as the *global* importance, in Fig. 11, of the information given about the Far East. (2)

10

Section 3

1. (a) What distinguishes the pattern of calorie-protein intake in the Far East since 1945?
   (b) What explanation does the writer offer for this state of affairs? (2)
2. From your reading of Figs. 10–13, supply the following information –
   (i) average daily protein intake, in grammes, of a Canadian?
   (ii) percentage of a Brazilian's diet that is carbohydrates?
   (iii) Africa's percentage share of the world's agricultural population?
   (iv) *excess* calorie intake of the average New Zealander?
   (v) the percentage of average West German's diet made up of fats?
   (vi) intake (in grammes) of sugar/sweet of a citizen of New York?
   (vii) the *difference* (in grammes) of the daily intake of fruit between a man in New York and one in Bombay? (7)

9

Section 4

(Based on Figs. 13 and 14 and relevant commentary)

1. Comment fully on the writer's use of the two dials to compare the daily diets of an American and an Indian. You should discuss the number of 'dots' and the position of the hands. (2)
2. Is P. W. Sukhatme's *The World's Hunger and Future Needs in Food Supplies* a *book* or an *article*? Give a reason for your answer. (2)
3. In what two respects do you find the statistic for protein intake (Fig. 14) in the Far East alarming? (1)
4. In Fig. 14, we see recorded a drop in calorie intake in two areas – the Far East and North America. Do you find both equally alarming? Explain your answer fully. (Look at Skills 1, 2, 3, 5, 8 and 12.) (2)

See page 44 for worked example.

5. Explain clearly, in your own words, what you understand by the following expressions – (i) "Pre-harvest void", (ii) "non-food", (iii) "the psychological satisfaction of mechanical eating". (5)

10

What Do People Need to Eat?

Passage 8, Section 4, Question 4.

In Fig. 14, we see recorded a drop in calorie intake in two areas – the Far East and North America. Do you find both equally alarming? Explain your answer fully. (2 marks)

Comment on requirements:
A question requiring some thought on the part of the reader. The pupil who confines himself to a study of Fig. 14 will learn nothing of value – to know whether the figures are alarming or not, he must know what they mean – and he can only discover that by relating the table in Fig. 14 to the rest of the passage. The title of the passage gives a useful clue.

Model answer:
The drop in the Far East's intake is much more alarming because even the first figure (. . . . . .) is less than the amount of protein required by people in . . . region, as it explains in Fig. 10.

In North America, even after the drop, people still take many more calories than they actually require. At the start of the passage it says that "the Far East calorie requirement is deficient by about 11 per cent" which means that they get a good lot less than they need.

Marker's comment:
The candidate has made sense of the figures in Fig. 14 by relating them to Fig. 10, and also to the opening of the passage. Notice that when he quotes he is careful to add an explanation in his own words as well.

9 Seeking Refuge

Behind the red door of a tiny terrace house off Peckham High Street, the sound of gongs and chanting is indistinctly to be heard on a Sunday afternoon. Inside the door, piles of discarded shoes fill the little hallway; the noise is louder, coming from an upstairs room. In that room, Indo-Chinese men and women squash closer together to make space for a European stranger; an orange-robed monk, shaven-headed, kneels and chants before a hugh painted Buddha.

This is the Vietnamese Buddhist Temple of London, a cell of colour and light in the wintry desert of south-east London. The room is vivid with wall hangings, paper streamers and lanterns, religious paintings; in every corner are placed little plates of fruit – oranges, pomegranates, grapes – and vases of flowers, both fresh and plastic. In the glow of many candles (wax and electric), the people kneel around their priest, eyes closed, their faces quiet in prayer; he sings alone but for the beating of the gong. It is a sad but prevailing sound: the music of a people in exile, far from home.

There are now some 19,000 Indo-Chinese refugees living in Britain who have come here in the decade since the end of the Vietnam war. They constitute an elusive community, masked by its smiling faces and its contradictory public images.

There is a face of success. Vietnamese entrepreneurs are selling fish and chips and Chinese chop suey from brightly painted take-away vans all over the country; a Vietnamese woman doctor has established a fashionable acupuncture practice in Cambridge; a Vietnamese schoolboy has been tipped to play football for Britain. But mainly the received images are darker ones. Refugees from Vietnam in Britain now, like Jews 40 years ago, have come to epitomise suffering and persecution of many sorts.

The Home Office itself has recently reported this as a fact to the House of Commons Home Affairs Sub-Committee on Race Relations and Immigration (SCORRI), rousing fleeting public concern just before last Christmas. 'In retrospect, the Vietnamese can clearly be seen as some of the most disadvantaged groups ever to come to the UK,' it declared, adding that the agencies working with them believed that 'while all refugees are prone to suffer some degree of tension and stress . . . the degree of stress and psychiatric illness among the Vietnamese is unparalleled'.

British local authorities have given them council flats and houses and some language and skills teaching. But the Government's policy of 'dispersal', designed to avoid ghettoes and undue pressure on particular local authorities, has scattered Vietnamese refugees in small numbers all over the country, sometimes as far north as Dundee (where they have experienced even the climate as punitive), and where they have often been too few for language or skills training to be successfully organised.

David Waddington, Home Office Minister, recently admitted while giving evidence to SCORRI that dispersal had proved 'a disaster' for the Vietnamese, isolated and immobilised as they already were by language problems.

Four years ago, community workers in south-east London were facing what they now admit was a'flashpoint situation' in the incidence of attacks on Vietnamese refugees. Families were stoned or beaten up as they tried to move into council flats; there were almost daily muggings, robberies, assaults on people or their homes. The aggressors were invariably white and right-wing. ('They'd have called themselves National Front, though they weren't capable of writing their names', said a social worker.)

The Observer Magazine, May 1985.

Passage 9

Section 1

1. Who is the writer of this extract?
   A. a Vietnamese businessman
   B. an Indo-Chinese refugee
   C. a "European stranger"
   D. an "orange-robed monk" (1)
2. The extract comes from one of the following:
   A. an information booklet for Vietnamese refugees
   B. a newspaper or magazine

C. a social worker's report
D. a government report (1)

3. The tone of the extract is generally what?
   A. sympathetic to the Vietnamese
   B. indifferent to the Vietnamese
   C. informative and unbiased
   D. anti-National Front (1)
4. Why did the Vietnamese refugees originally come to this country? (1)
5. Paragraph 1 outlines a sort of journey.
   (a) Describe the stages of the journey in your own words.
   (b) Suggest a reason why the writer begins this way. (4)
6. What overall impression of the Indo-Chinese refugees do we gain from reading the first two paragraphs? (2)

10

Section 2

1. Give two reasons why the word "cell" (line 7) might be considered an appropriate way to describe this temple. (2)
2. Why does the music of the gong seem to the writer to be particularly apt? (1)
3. In line 17 the writer uses the word "masked" rather than, say, 'hidden.' Suggest a reason why he chose this particular word. (1)
4. (a) What are the two contrasting pictures of the refugees outlined in paragraph 4?
   (b) Which does the writer think is the commoner image? (3)
5. What *is* SCORRI? (1)
6. Explain in your own words the meaning of the phrase "one of the most disadvantaged groups". (1)
7. Why is the section from "In retrospect . . . . is unparalleled" in (lines 28–33) in inverted commas? (1)

10

Section 3

1. (a) Outline the contrast contained in the first sentence of paragraph 2.
   (b) How does the next sentence elaborate on one of the ideas?
   (c) Comment on the writer's use of "fresh and plastic" and "wax and electric" to contribute to the contrast in this paragraph. (4)
2. Explain what you think the writer means by "elusive community" and say how the context helped you arrive at this conclusion. (2)
3. The word "dispersal" (line 35) describes government policy regarding the distribution of Vietnamese refugees in Britain. Explain clearly, (a) what this policy involved, and (b) why it has proved a disaster. (4)

10

Section 4

1. When refugees were sent to Dundee they "experienced even the climate as punitive." Explain clearly what the writer means here, bringing out the impact of the word "even" on the meaning. (2)

2. Examine the context of the word "entrepreneurs" (line 19) and show how this helps you to arrive at the meaning of the word. (2)

3. Explain how people could be "isolated and immobilised" by language problems. (line 43)
(Look at Skills 1, 2, 3, 8, 9 and 12.) (2)

See below for worked example.

4. What is meant by the term "right-wing" (line 48)? (1)
5. Examine the whole passage carefully, trying to identify the devices used by the writer to give an air of authority and a feeling of expertise to his writing, so that the reader will think, "Well, this man is an expert. He knows his stuff."
   Refer to, and comment on, at least **four** such devices, making it clear which one you personally found most convincing. (5)

10

Seeking Refuge

Passage 9, Section 4, Question 3.

Explain how people could be "isolated and immobilised" by language problems. (line 43) (2 marks)

Comment on requirements:
There are two stages to this question. The first involves the distinction between "isolated" and "immobilised". The second involves relating both these words to "language problems".

Model answer:
Isolated means cut off, like an island cut off from the mainland. Immobilised means unable to move.

If people do not understand the language of a country very well, they are cut off from the people around them. They are also stuck, not able to move; they cannot make progress in any direction until they make progress in the language. Likewise they are unable to make any progress, like getting a good job, until progress is made in the language. It is as if you are on an island with no way of getting off.

Marker's comment:
A thorough answer, although the candidate tends to repeat himself to make his point clear. He makes the distinction between the two words, and he illustrates that application to language problems with examples.

10 The Talking Shop of the World

'The hard realities of world politics . . . blew in the door before the workmen had finished'
Trygve Lie, first Secretary-General

2 **'The UN has been largely ignored and defied'**
Javier Pérez de Cuellar, 1989 Secretary-General

3 **'What we do should have the support . . . of plain men'**
Dag Hammarskjold, second Secretary-General

4 **'One of the most important roles of the UN is that of a figure at which things can be thrown with impunity'**
U Thant, third Secretary-General

The United Nations was founded by the winners of the world's worst war who were terrified of war and wanted to stop war. Out of terror, idealism and a curiously narrow view of the future management of the world, they framed the UN charter in San Francisco in 1945, expressing the determination to end "the scourge of war" and to "live as good neighbours".

In that principal objective the UN has failed. It has held up a mirror to the vanities, foolishness and obsessions of men and the complexities of a world vastly different from the one its founders knew. That it endures is testimony to the resilience of hope and the need for a talking shop.

While some scorn it as a tedious babel, a dustbin for insoluble problems, a platform for ranters, a place as irritating as a smoky chimney, it is never theless regarded as an indispensable workshop, the world's meeting place and schoolroom, where problems are endlessly massaged and sometimes alleviated.

Of course, the debates in the narrow glass tower on international territory in Manhattan are only the iceberg's tip. Much of the UN's work is out of the headlines: its vast worldwide network has beaten smallpox and improved the living conditions, food, education and health of billions of people. In human rights it has made the private cruelty of governments a public matter.

The original question – what is the UN for? – remains as relevant today as in 1945. This and the record of occasional successes and numerous failures are part of its inherent contradictions and endless paradoxes. The very name, United Nations, seems at times a mockery. The world pretends it wants it to do much, while allowing it to do little.

The Times, October 23, 1985.

Passage 10

Section 1

1. List the names of the Secretaries-General of the UN in chronological order. (2)
2. Give the number of the photograph of the present Secretary-General. (1)
3. (i) In what year was the UN Charter framed?
   (ii) In what city was it framed?
   (iii) What does the word "framed" mean? (3)
4. This article was written to commemorate the . . . . . . anniversary of the UN. Supply the missing word. (1)
5. From the sound and appearance of their *names*, see if you can give the names of the Secretary General who was (a) South American, (b) Asian. (2)
6. Look at the quoted comments of the Secretaries-General. Which one (give the number of the photograph) suggested that it was perhaps the UN's role to be a universal Aunt Sally? (1)

10

Section 2

(Based on paragraph 4)

1. Quote the expression that describes the architectural appearance of the UN building. (1)
2. In your own words explain what **two** facts we are given about its location. (2)
3. What two things does the expression "the tip of the iceberg" normally suggest about the properties of icebergs? (2)
4. What, in the passage, is the writer describing as the "iceberg's tip"? (1)
5. What, in terms of the work of the UN, is the rest of the iceberg? (paragraph 4) (1)

   See page 51 for worked example.
6. What three positive achievements has the rest of the UN iceberg accomplished? You may quote the first two, but must give the third in your own words. (4)

10

Section 3

1. What, according to the writer, was the "world's worst war"? (1)
2. What was the principal objective of the UN? (1)
3. What two things, according to the writer, has it done instead? (2)
4. For what two reasons, therefore, does he consider it has survived? (2)
5. In your own words, carefully avoiding the given figures of speech, give the reasons why people tend to despise the UN. (4)

10

Section 4

1. Although people despise the UN, the writer sees it as fulfilling three functions – workshop, meeting place and schoolroom. Write a sentence explaining clearly what useful purpose is suggested by each image. (3)
2. Bring out clearly the distinction between problems that are "endlessly massaged" and problems "sometimes alleviated". (3)
3. Show how the immediate context helps you to define the word "paradox". (2)
4. In your own words, explain the two paradoxes the writer uses to illustrate his point. (2)

10

The Talking Shop of the World

Passage 10, Section 2, Question 5.

What, in terms of the work of the UN, is the rest of the iceberg? (paragraph 4) (1 mark)

Comment on requirements:
Note that the question refers to a specific paragraph, so concentrate on that; it also follows on from the previous question, so consider the answer to that also. Note also that the question says "in terms of the work of the UN", so that it will not be enough simply to say "the other work they do apart from debates".

Model answer:
The rest of the iceberg is the bit you don't see. With the UN, it is the enormous amount of work they do that never makes front page news.

Marker's comment:
The pupil does well to explain his answer in terms of the image, and he is also careful to gloss the term that occurs in the passage. "Out of the headlines" becomes "never makes front page news".

11 Thirty Minutes to Stop the Holocaust

This is the nightmare. At 07.00 hours GMT a fleet of 2000 rockets rise from their silos in the Soviet Union. Four minutes later the ICBMS (intercontinental ballistic missiles) are out in space, above the earth's atmosphere, heading for the United States. Their paths curve. Suddenly each rocket drops away, leaving a "bus" – a container loaded with warheads and decoys. The bus is left just above the North Pole. At 07.11 the bus unloads.

The warheads, each carrying a computer that directs it to its own target, are released. So are a much larger number of decoys. All are still travelling in space. Three minutes later they aren't. The decoys are doing whatever they will and the warheads are falling through the earth's atmosphere to their targets. We are now in the "terminal phase". The entire process, the first half of a nuclear war, has taken 29 minutes, a breakfast time for man but at 07.29 the beginning of the end for mankind.

Or is it? For the first time the nuclear threat that has hung over our heads for most of our lifetimes may be about to be removed: this is the power and the glory claimed for the star wars defence system – a claim that is as disputed as it is superlative, creating inter-continental divisions among political allies, working scientists, military strategists and academic researchers.

Under star wars that 29-minute scenario will never happen. Instead the following

is postulated. At 07.00 hours the Russian rockets take off. They continue to blast out flames and hot gases triggered by their ignition under ground. They begin their journey slowly. They are now vulnerable to weapons. During the "boost phase", the first three or four minutes before the rockets reach the relative safety of space, their heat emissions are detected by a surveillance satellite. This in turn alerts a space gunship – an orbiting satellite armed with chemical laser guns. Like something out of a space movie or a computer game, the rockets are then simply "zapped" from outer space. Most important of all, the multiple warheads and decoys are still during this critical boost phase in the head of the rocket. They are zapped, too.

There are alternative attacks during the boost phase. American rockets carrying laser guns are unleashed from submarines. They travel fast enough to overtake the ICBMs before they leave the earth's atmosphere. The laser guns pop up, the enemy is zapped.

Other star wars weapons would be brought into play. A giant orbiting mirror is used to reflect beams aimed from earthbound lasers. The mirror is of an accuracy so as not to dilute the laser beam's intensity. The beams, which are under computer control, are focused on the moving enemy. Each beam zaps one rocket. If, for whatever reason, the Russian weapons are still on course, the missiles and the decoys will at 07.27 leave the relative safety of space and return to earth's atmosphere.

They are now poised to strike the United States. Heated by friction, they become visible to a space-based heat sensor. This alerts a battle station, also orbiting in space, which fires a "neutral particle beam". Neutral particles are atoms which have no electrical charge; they destroy the vital micro-chip at the heart of the ICBM's electronic system. In the final minutes of the terminal phase there remains yet one more defiant rather old-fashioned option for the Americans to hurl at the invader. These are "smart rocks" – guided missiles launched from an aircraft to attack the missiles. At 07.29 by star wars time, the enemy attack has been repelled. The nuclear holocaust has been averted.

Passage 11

Section 1

1. In this "war game", which country is (a) the attacker, and (b) the attacked? (2)
2. Explain clearly – (a) 07.00 hours GMT and (b) 07.29 star wars time. (2)
3. Give a reason why the writer begins with such a short sentence. (1)
4. Quote from the passage **four** words or expressions that are in inverted commas because they are examples of star wars' *jargon*. (2)
5. Quote from the passage a word that is in inverted commas but is *not* jargon. Why is this word in inverted commas? (2)
6. Explain the word "scenario". (1)

10

Section 2

1. There are four stages in an ICBM's progress towards its target. From your reading of the passage, briefly outline these four stages. (N.B. You should *not* write about American weapons.) (4)
2. Copy down this simple chart. In the space opposite each item listed, say what its function in the star wars' scenario is to be, using your own words as far as possible.

Silo	
Decoy	
Surveillance Satellite	
Giant Orbiting Mirror	
Neutral Particle Beam	
Space-Based Heat Sensor	

(6)

10

Section 3

1. How are war heads guided to their targets? (1)
2. What is the most "old fashioned" way of destroying rockets? (1)
3. "the relative safety of space" – Give **two** reasons why space, for an aggressor, is safer than the earth's atmosphere. (2)
4. "a claim that is as disputed as it is superlative."
   (a) in your own words explain what this means.
   (b) Do you think the *writer* would dispute the star wars' scenario? Give a reason for your opinion. (4)
5. What linking purpose does the sentence "Or is it?" serve in the passage? (paragraph 3) (2)

   See page 55 for worked example.
6. Explain fully how the context of the word "terminal" in the last paragraph helped you to arrive at its meaning. (2)

10

Section 4

1. Comment, in a sentence on each, on the effectiveness of the writer's use of the following –

(a) "At 07.11 the bus unloads."
(b) "the power and the glory"
(c) "pop up" (6)

2. The final sentence in paragraph 2 echoes Neil Armstrong's words when he first landed on the moon:
"One small step for a man, but a giant leap for mankind."
Explain fully one *similarity* and one *contrast* that you feel the writer might want you to consider because of the echo. (4)

10

Thirty Minutes to Stop the Holocaust

Passage 11, Section 3, Question 5.

What linking purpose does the sentence "Or is it?" serve in the passage? (paragraph 3) (2 marks)

Comment on requirements:
A link joins two things, in this case parts of the passage – so look to see what the parts *before* and *after* the sentence are about.

Model answer:
The first part of the passage says how a nuclear attack would happen without "star wars" technology. It ends by saying that 07.29 is "the beginning of the end for mankind".

The author then casts doubt on this by asking "Or is it?" and goes on to answer his question in the second part, which says how the same attack would go with "star wars". That part ends "at 07.29 star war time, the enemy attack has been repelled."

Marker's comment:
There are two important things here: what distinguishes the two parts of the passage, and what relates them.

The pupil has seen that what distinguishes the parts is that the second deals with the effect of "star wars" technology on the situation described in the first. What relates them is the given sentence "Or is it?" which questions the conclusions of the first part and prepares for the answer provided by the second. The pupil has done well to use quotations to support his answer.

12 Four Minutes to Midnight

Human beings strive for consistency in their affairs. They cannot – at least they cannot for long – hold incompatible beliefs. Either, it seems, we look to the right of the picture or else to the left. Either we believe the world is threatened by extinction, or else we don't. How can we at one and the same time declare ourselves for human rights, devote ourselves to our children, labour to produce lasting works of art and scholarship . . . *and* take seriously a vision of the future in which there are no children, in which our books will never be read, and our paintings, our houses, our flower-gardens will end as dust? One or the other vision has to go.

Let us not be deceived. The dangers will not be diminished because we close our eyes to them. If we cannot carry on as normal under the shadow of the Bomb, then for the time being we have a duty *not* to carry on as normal. We live at a time when to deny the prospect of death may well cost us our lives.

Yet try telling that to other people. Try telling it in Gath and publishing it in the streets of Askelon . . . for the attitude of the daughters of the Philistines is little changed. To speak the truth among people who do not want to hear it is considered almost an aggressive act – an invasion of privacy, a trespass into someone else's space. Not nice, not done . . .

A year ago in Pennsylvania, USA, eight nuclear protesters who called themselves the Plowshares 8 (they included two priests, a nun, a lawyer and a professor of history) broke into a weapons factory and damaged the nose-cone of a Mark 12 missile with a hammer. They were accused at their trial of burglary, criminal conspiracy and trespass. Each faced a maximum sentence of twenty-five years. 'This time', the prosecution said, 'you've gone too far.' They *had* gone too far, they *had* trespassed: but their trespass was not so much against the property of the General Electric Company as against the minds of the American public. By

attacking the missile with a hammer they were forcing other people to think, however briefly, about a subject regarded as indecent – the question of just what such a missile might be for.

Their behaviour was Embarrassing. Not nice. Niceness can be a virtue. Most of us are nice people – we will not put other people out of countenance if we can help it, we will not deliberately rob them of comforting illusions. But niceness can be a dreadful vice as well. Here is what Heinrich Himmler had to say in a speech in 1943: 'In public we will never talk about it . . . It is with us, thank God, an inborn gift of tactfulness, that we have never conversed about this matter, never spoken about it . . . I am referring to the extermination of the Jewish people.' Indeed Himmler did not refer, in public, to the 'extermination of the Jewish people': words like 'special treatment' were made to serve instead.

The Nazis, however, were not alone in their anxiety to avoid plain speaking. The victims did so too. We find certain elders of the Jewish community referring to the trains which took their brothers and sisters to the killing centres as 'favoured transport'; even in Auschwitz a crematorium would be called a 'bakery'.

And now? Who can avoid the parallel with our own situation, and the tricks of language which good taste and good form impose upon discussions – at least official discussions – of the Bomb? For 'special treatment' read 'demographic targeting', for 'bakery' read 'domestic fall-out shelter'.

But it would be wrong to pretend that it is only our own decent reticence which restrains us from breaking the taboos. We will – and we are generally quite well aware of it – be made to pay a public price for 'going too far'. When other people do not want to know, they *do not want to know* – and they do not take kindly to the self-appointed prophet who sees it as his duty to inform them.

In the old days it is said that kings would kill the messenger who brought bad news. Today, in the United States, the messenger may, as almost happened to the Plowshares 8, be silenced by the law; in Russia he may get locked up in a mental hospital. But there are other and subtler ways of restraining those who might otherwise speak out. And in our own country none is better tried or more effective than the technique of the social pillory. Anyone who forces an unwanted confrontation on the subject of the Bomb is liable to be punished for his impudence by being mocked, snubbed, made the butt of sneers and ridicule.

We all know the standard vocabulary of put-downs. 'Idealist', 'pacificist', 'moralist', 'holier-than-thou'. They have been with us a long time. The same schoolboy insults which Winston Churchill used to disparage those who objected to the idea of using anthrax bombs in the last war – 'psalm-singing defeatists' Churchill called them – have now been dusted off by the brave editors of the *Daily This* or *Morning That* for use against our nuclear disarmers. And in settings where such clichés might be seen for what they are, cleverer men can be counted on to produce cleverer but equally dismissive sneers. Alistair Cooke, for example, writing about Bertrand Russell in the *Manchester Guardian* some years ago: 'A midget suspended against a huge Cinemascope screen . . . a charming puppet straining for a miracle and in the act wobbling the tiny wire frame of his body . . . "It is", he said in his high nasal voice, "the most important question men have ever had to decide in the whole history of the human race."' A clever insult? Yes, a clever insult whereby a man who has shown too much emotion is defined as a puppet, a doll without emotions.

Lord Russell, peer of the realm and the greatest philosopher in England, was surely able to weather this kind of abuse. But few of us have Russell's social or intellectual confidence. Hardly surprising, then, if we sometimes persuade ourselves that, whatever we think privately, it is just not our place to make a public stand against the Bomb. Lords, philosophers, actresses, priests . . . they do that kind of thing. They can make exhibitions of themselves. But for the rest of us? Well, on the whole, all things considered, we like to keep calm. It is not our way to scream, or sing psalms, or call things the most important question in the whole history of the human race – even when the water is lapping round our feet. First one to panic is a wet.

Passage 12

Section 1

In this section, all you are required to do is write down the letter of the answer that you think is the best response to the question.

1. The writer's *main* argument is . .?

   A. the Bomb is useful and worthwhile
   B. the Bomb has proved itself an effective deterrent
   C. people don't think or do enough about the Bomb
   D. it's better not to get involved in political matters

2. The Plowshares 8 broke into . .?

   A. head office of the General Electric Company
   B. a plant for making weapons
   C. a government military base
   D. CND headquarters in Askelon

3. Himmler was . .?

   A. against the extermination of the Jews
   B. for the extermination of the Jews
   C. just obeying orders
   D. not involved and didn't care one way or the other

4. Bertrand Russell was . .?

   A. a puppet
   B. a supporter of the Bomb
   C. editor of the *Manchester Guardian*
   D. a nobleman and thinker

5. Winston Churchill was . . .?

   A. a supporter of the objectors to using anthrax
   B. hostile to those who objected to the use of anthrax
   C. kept in the dark about it by his military advisors
   D. believed that ordinary people should decide for themselves

6. The writer thinks that . .?

   A. protest is wrong
   B. we should all protest if we feel we ought to
   C. there's no point in protesting
   D. we should leave it to famous people like lords, philosophers, actresses.

7. The Plowshares 8's real crime, according to the writer, was . .?

   A. making people think about something they preferred not to think about
   B. trespass
   C. damaging government property
   D. indecent behaviour

8. The writer mentions the occupations of members of Plowshares 8 to . . . .?

   A. suggest they were all religious people
   B. suggest they were all professional people
   C. suggest they were the last sort of people one would expect to indulge in such illegal behaviour
   D. suggest they had been conned by someone else into doing this sort of thing

9. The writer brings in the Nazis because . . .?

   A. the Nazis also understood the importance of using language to conceal rather than communicate
   B. historically, the Nazis had almost discovered the Bomb themselves
   C. they knew how to deal with people like Plowshares 8
   D. because Himmler was a Nazi

10. Jewish elders referred to the trains as 'favoured transport' because . . .?

   A. the trains were subsidised by the government
   B. they were far superior to buses and especially lorries
   C. they wanted to fool the other Jews
   D. they needed to disguise from themselves the reality they needed

___
10

Section 2

1. In your opinion, why does the writer use 'we' and 'us' so often in his argument? (1)
2. Justify the writer's use of the capital letters at 'Bomb' (line 11) and 'Embarrassing' (line 30) (2)
3. Look at the words in inverted commas (lines 45–46)
   Why are these expressions in inverted commas?
   Give the *source* of each expression. (3)
4. Explain in your own words why the insult, (line 72) was "a clever insult". (2)
5. Look at paragraph 1. Here the writer lists items that people want in this world. Select **one**, and in greater detail, explain how it fits into the writer's argument. (2)

___
10

Section 3

1. "Human beings strive for consistency in their affairs."
   Explain how the author develops this argument in the rest of paragraph 1. (2)
2. "We live at a time when to deny the prospect of death may well cost us our lives."
   What is unusual about the wording of this expression?
   Explain what the writer means by it. (3)
3. What are the advantages and disadvantages of "niceness"?
   Why, in your view, has the writer chosen this particular word?
   (Look at Skills 2, 3, 9, 10 and 11.) (3)

   See page 61 for worked example.
4. What point does the writer make about the effect "niceness" has on our choice of expression? Why is this such an important point? (2)
5. What, according to the writer, enabled Bertrand Russell to cope better with such insults? (2)
6. Comment on the writer's use of the word "wet" in the final sentence. (1)

10

Section 4

1. "Holier-than-thou" and "psalm-singing defeatist" are two insults mentioned by the writer.
   What *connection* do these have?
   In what way does this contribute to the insulting nature of the expression? (2)
2. "the brave editors of the *Daily This* or *Morning That*"
   What is the writer's attitude to the editors?
   How is his attitude strengthened by the choice of newspaper titles? (2)
3. "*under the shadow of* the Bomb"
   Give **two** possible ideas suggested by the choice of expression. (2)
4. (a) Explain what the author means by "social pillory".
   (b) When, according to the writer, is this used? (2)
5. Explain in your own words why "helplessness" is "a self-confirming process." (2)

10

Four Minutes to Midnight

Passage 12, Section 3, Question 3.

> What are the advantages and disadvantages of "niceness"?
> Why, in your view, has the writer chosen this particular word?
> (3 marks)

Comment on requirements:
The allocation of marks here suggests three separate areas to consider:
1) advantages, 2) disadvantages, 3) reasons for choice of this word.

Model answer:
The author says that "niceness can be a virtue . . . but can be a dreadful vice." Niceness is a good thing in normal circumstances because it involves considering other people's feelings, and not hurting or embarrassing them with the truth; e.g. pretending to like a hairstyle which you think is awful. But in some cases the truth is more important than other people's feelings and then "niceness" is a bad thing because it stops us speaking out when we ought to.

I think this word was chosen because it has associations with a particular way of life that many lead, where some subjects are 'not nice' and so never get talked about – like death or going to the toilet. In the passage, the author sees "niceness" as one of the main things that prevent us from facing the truth about nuclear weapons.

Marker's comment:
An understanding of this question is vital to the argument of the passage as a whole. The pupil has proved that he understands the author's argument by giving examples of his own, and he has drawn extensively on his own experience to answer the question, but he is careful to relate it to the passage at the end.

Unit 2

READING SKILLS:

Varied Exercises

Introduction

In this unit there are opportunities to apply different kinds of reading skills and techniques to a variety of verbal and visual extracts, and to have fun in the process. Activities like sequencing (passages 5 and 8) or cloze procedure (passage 6) can be treated as games, although they do have the serious intention of revealing features of language, vocabulary and meaning.

1 Top of the Class

PERCENTAGE OF ECONOMICALLY ACTIVE AND RETIRED PEOPLE IN EACH SOCIAL CLASS IN GREAT BRITAIN DEVISED FROM CENSUS, 1971

SOCIAL CLASS 1 – Professional – 4%
Accountants, chemists, university dons, lawyers, vets, opticians, ornithologists, scientists, vicars, engineers, architects, dentists.

SOCIAL CLASS II – Intermediate occupations – 18%
Airline pilots, chiropodists, farmers, members of parliament, schoolmasters, police inspectors, artists, nurses, publicans, journalists, sculptors, diplomats, chicken sexers, actors, company directors.

SOCIAL CLASS III (*N*) – Skilled occupations – Non Manual – 21%
Sales reps, secretaries, shop girls, bank clerks, photographers, restaurateurs, policemen, cashiers, models, undertakers.

SOCIAL CLASS III (*M*) – Skilled occupations – Manual – 28%
Bus drivers, cooks, miners, guards in trains, upholsterers, butchers, all athletes including horseback riders and foot-ballers, plumbers, shoemakers, printers, brewers.

SOCIAL CLASS IV Partly skilled – 21%
Farm labourers, barmen, bus conductors, fishermen, postmen, telephonists, milk-men, gardeners, hawkers, ambulance men, barmaids, brewers, waiters and waitresses.

SOCIAL CLASS V – Unskilled – 8%
Office cleaners, porters, builders' labourers, messenger boys, lorry drivers' mates, stevedores, window cleaners, chimney sweeps, ticket collectors, charwomen.

Talking

1. Most people prefer to divide society into the upper, middle and working classes. How would these divisions relate to the above information?
2. According to these details what social class do you and your parents belong to? Is this the same class you thought?
3. The most common way of determining a person's class is to look at the job he or she does. How satisfactory do you find this a way of defining class? Do you, for example, agree that vicars should be in social class I but company directors in social class II?

Reading

1. Can you think of any good reason for the relatively high grading (II) of chicken-sexers?

2. Does the recruiting slogan, *Join the Professionals*, persuade you that *all* soldiers should be in Class I?
3. How would a girl who was a secretary in a high-class hotel react to being given the same status as an assistant in a small shop?
4. Would Dr David Owen do better to be graded as a doctor or a politician?
5. In what skills is a hawker (Grade IV) "partly skilled"?

Into which grade would you assign the following, accepting the given terms?

a disc jockey

Ian Botham

fashion designer

second-hand car salesman

Army sergeant-major

millionaire pop singer

lavatory attendant

carpenter (self-employed)

professional burglar

judge

According to the census details, into which social class do the following fall? Write down each name and beside it the social group.
State then if you feel that person might (a) be pleased or (b) object strongly.
What, do you think, would be the basis of their pleasure or objection?

Steve Davis

Paul McCartney

Esther Rantzen

David Attenborough

Sebastian Coe

John Cleese

2 Finding Your Feet . . . in Colchester

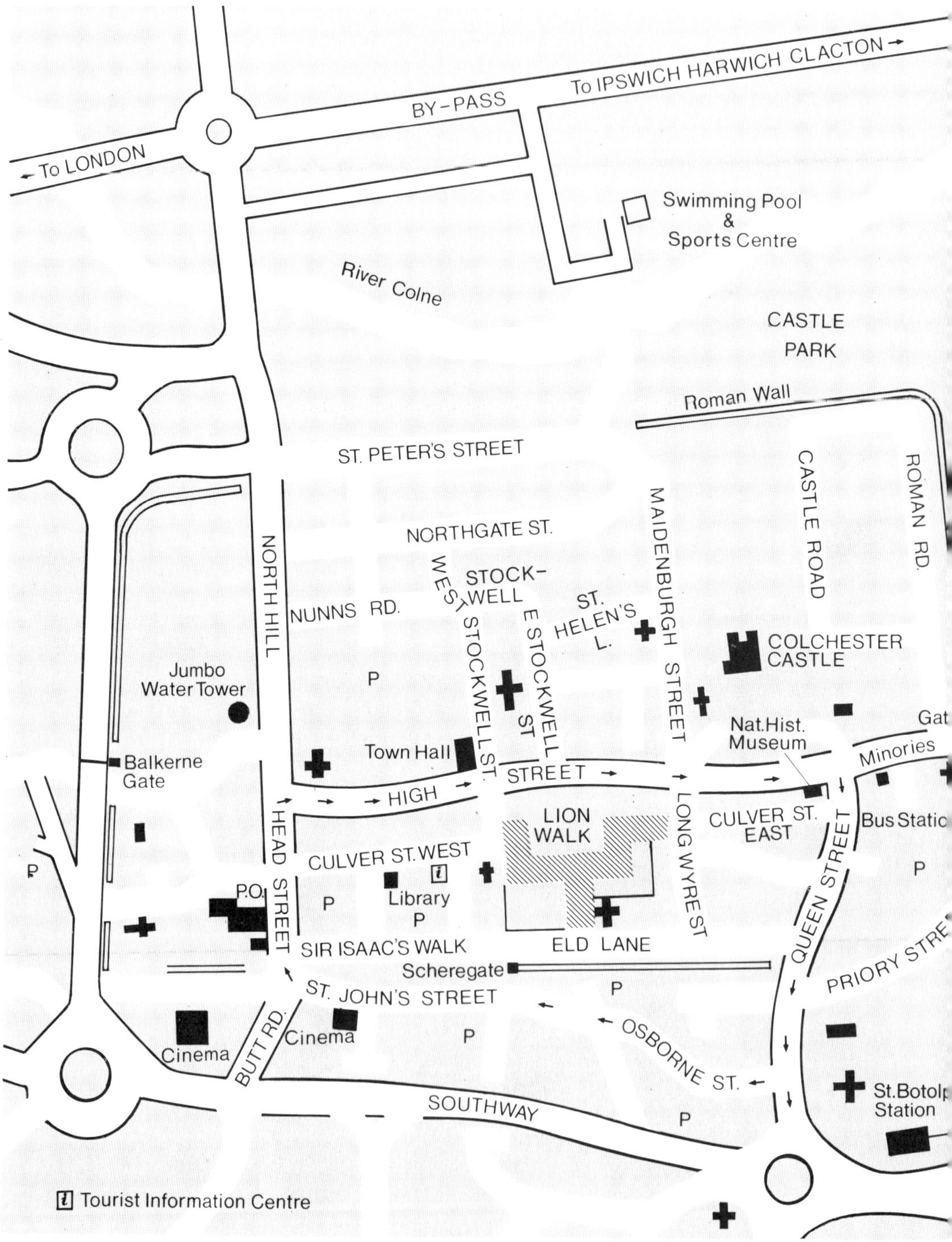

1. What is the best route to get you from the Post Office to the Tourist Information Centre *by car*?
2. Now you've found out what Colchester has to offer, you decide to *walk* from the Tourist Information Centre to the Natural History Museum. Describe what route you take.
3. Sadly, the Natural History Museum is closed so you decide to walk to the River Colne. What route do you take and what buildings of interest might you see?
4. You have a picnic beside the river and then decide to stroll round the town walls. There are three places where the sites of the gates in the old wall can be seen. Name one of the surviving gates. How do you know there was a fourth gate?
5. On your walk you have seen these three buildings:
   a) the Jumbo Water Tower
   b) St. Botolph's Station
   c) the Swimming Pool and Sports Centre
   Which of them is in the oldest part of the town? Give a reason for your answer.
6. How many churches stand in the old Roman town?
7. You fancy a visit to the St John's Street cinema. Assuming you can park outside, what route do you take with your car if you start from the Natural History Museum? If you start from the Library, is it quicker to drive or walk? Give a reason for your answer.
8. Emerging from the cinema, you find that your car has finally broken down. Thoroughly fed up, you decide to leave Colchester by train. What's the best route by foot from the cinema to the station?
9. As you queue for your ticket you wonder why the station has got such an odd name. What name has it got? Why does it have this name?

3 Square Leg

"Square Leg" was the name given to the 1980 Home Defence exercise. The envisaged attack was 131 warheads (62 air bursts and 69 ground bursts) totalling 205 megatons on a mixture of military and city targets.

1979 Population of Britain: 54 million (each figure = 1 million)

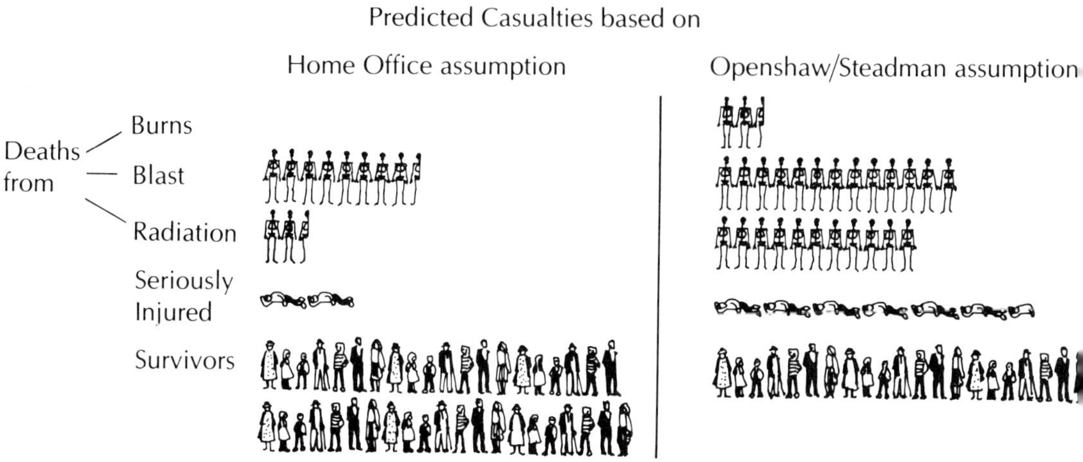

1. Why has the artist chosen to represent the population in this way?
2. What is gained by having the Home Office assumption and that of Openshaw/Steadman assumption side by side?
3. Broadly, what differences are there between the two assumptions? What reasons can you think of for these differences? Why are they called "assumptions"?
4. Why has the artist chosen different figures for each category? Why these particular ones? How effective do you find them?
5. What category of death is missing from the Home Office Assumption? Why do you think it is missing?
6. How many deaths by radiation are there in a) the Home Office assumption, b) the Openshaw/Steadman assumption?
7. How many *total* deaths in a) the Home Office assumption, b) the Openshaw/Steadman assumption?
8. Why are the seriously injured not counted among the survivors?
9. How many *more* seriously wounded injured are there in the Openshaw/Steadman assumption?
10. How many survivors does each assumption claim there will be?
11. This diagram comes from a book about nuclear war. From the evidence of the diagram what attitudes do the writers have towards nuclear war? Explain why you have attributed these attitudes to them.
12. What is served by presenting the information in diagram form? Are there any disadvantages of using this method?
13. What does the information in the diagram add to your *knowledge* about nuclear war? How, if at all, does it effect your *attitudes*?

4 True/False?

Shares of total national post-tax income secured by the rich, the middle class and the poor.

Groups of income recipients	Share of total national post-tax income at: 1949 (%)	1957 (%)	1963 (%)	1967 (%)	1970 (%)	1972 (%)
the richest 10%	**27.1**	**24.0**	**25.2**	**24.3**	**21.5**	**22.0**
the middle 60%	**58.3**	**62.5**	**63.0**	**63.7**	**63.8**	**65.5**
the poorest 30%	**14.6**	**13.4**	**11.8**	**12.0**	**14.7**	**12.5**

Sources. For 1949–67, National Income and Expenditure Blue Books; for 1970, Inland Revenue Statistics 1972, table 57, for 1972, Family Expenditure Survey, tables 1 and 32.

Reading

Look at the table above and say whether the following statements are *true* or *false*.

1. By 1972 only the middle class had improved their share of national income since 1949.
2. The richest 10% had their lowest share of national income in 1972.
3. The poorest 30% had a larger share in 1949 than at any time to 1972.
4. In 1963 the richest 10% gained a larger share than in 1957 at the expense of the poorest class.
5. The rich had a greater share of national income in 1967 than they had in 1957.
6. The poorest class had their lowest share of national income in 1957.
7. The poorest class always received less than half their share of national income (assuming equal shares for all).
8. In 1972 the middle classes had improved on their 1949 share at the expense of both other classes.
9. In 1970 the poorest had improved on their share at the expense of the middle classes.
10. The middle classes increased their share most dramatically between 1970–2.

5 Di's Dad Pays for Dead Dog

Sequencing

1. Rewrite this newspaper item, putting the 'jumbled up' bits back in order.
2. When you have done so, write the code order of letters, attached to each bit, in the correct order.

A A judge said yesterday: "Plainly the Earl knew nothing about it."

B Earl Spencer and two of his gamekeepers were sued after the valuable pedigree was shot on his estate.

C "But he must stand or fall by what his employees have done."

D Princess Di's dad must pay £1000 over a dead dog.

E Mr Smith said he knew nothing about it.

F The action, in Northampton Crown Court, was raised by Jo Green, whose Rottweiler bitch Elka vanished while out for a morning run with two other dogs.

G During the search, her friend, business man Mark Shine, asked keeper Tony Smith, 40, if he had seen the dog.

H Elka's body was burned in a forestry fire.

I In court, Mr Smith said he ordered an assistant William Linford to shoot Elka and another dog in a spinney on the Althorp estate because they were chasing young pheasants.

J Miss Green said later: "I'm delighted with the verdict. I was particularly fond of Elka. If the personalities involved had been straight from the start, it need not have come to this."

K Judge John MacGregor said Mr Smith had explained his deliberate lie by saying "It was policy to say nothing to anyone about the estate because of a certain well-known member of the family".

6 Lonely

Each number enclosed within brackets represents a *single word* omitted from the passage.

Supply the missing words, making sure that each word fits in with (a) the continuing sense of the passage, and (b) the grammatical structure from which it has been omitted.

As the days passed into weeks, and the (1) passed into months, I began to wonder (2) Mark Lynch did not come to see me.

To begin with, I had not thought anything of it, but (3) his neglect seemed strange; for I realised suddenly that (4) had seen more of him than of (5) else at the art school.

When I had first gone (6) I had known nobody; and my evenings in my room on Croom's Hill were spent all (7). I used to come back and climb the stairs and throw myself down on the bed, sprawling out my legs and burying my face in the pillow. I would be thinking of the pleasures and the (8) in the day that had just passed. Then, turning over, I would stare at the uneven ceiling and wonder how (9) longer my life would lack direction, how much (10) I would be cut (11) yet searching for my true place in the world. I (12) of the hours wasted at the art school, with the drawing-board in front of me and the pencil in my (13), the feeling of uselessness that came upon me as I sat there, staring into space.

It was always a relief and a pleasure to reach the (14) of the day, when I would go down to the refectory, buy an enormous shortbread biscuit wrapped in silver paper, and sit eating it alone at the far end of one of the long tables. I would have beside me a glass of very hot milky coffee from which I took sips (15) and then.

7 I Sent a Letter to My Love . . .

Here are two short love letters, written in the late sixteenth century. The lovers have had a bit of a tiff but . . . . .

Rewrite the two letters, keeping the sense and sequence of the originals, but modernising the language so that your finished letters read as if they had been written by a couple of your contemporaries.

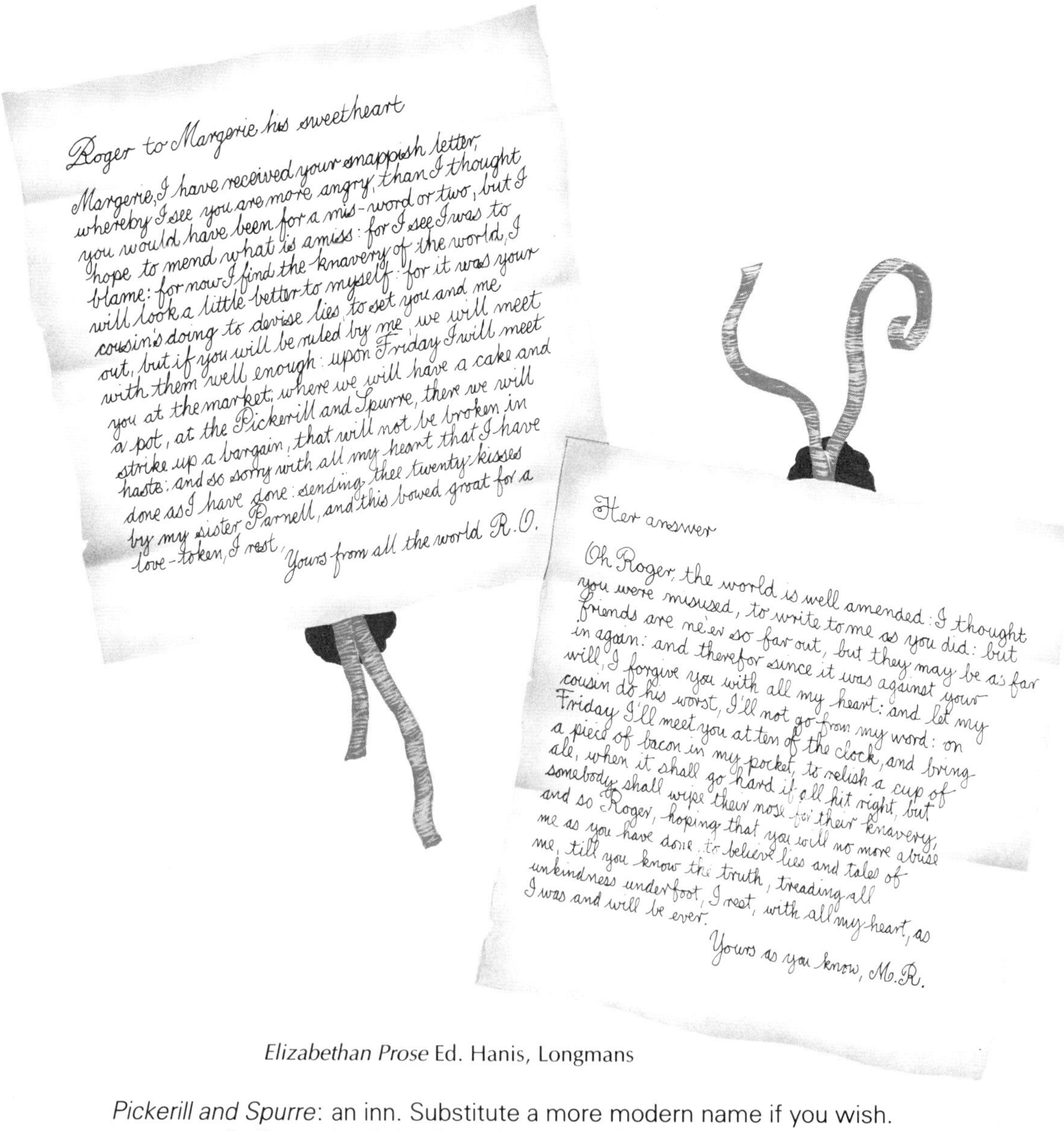

Roger to Margerie his sweetheart

Margerie, I have received your snappish letter, whereby I see you are more angry than I thought you would have been for a mis-word or two, but I hope to mend what is amiss: for I see I was to blame: for now I find the knavery of the world, I will look a little better to myself: for it was your cousin's doing to devise lies to set you and me out, but if you will be ruled by me, we will meet with them well enough: upon Friday I will meet you at the market, where we will have a cake and a pot, at the Pickerill and Spurre, there we will strike up a bargain, that will not be broken in haste: and so sorry with all my heart that I have done as I have done: sending thee twenty kisses by my sister Parnell, and this bowed groat for a love-token, I rest,

Yours from all the world R.O.

Her answer

Oh Roger, the world is well amended: I thought you were misused, to write to me as you did: but friends are ne'er so far out, but they may be as far in again: and therefor since it was against your will, I forgive you with all my heart: and let my cousin do his worst, I'll not go from my word: on Friday I'll meet you at ten of the clock, and bring a piece of bacon in my pocket, to relish a cup of ale, when it shall go hard if all hit right, but somebody shall wipe their nose for their knavery, and so Roger, hoping that you will no more abuse me as you have done, to believe lies and tales of me, till you know the truth, treading all unkindness underfoot, I rest, with all my heart, as I was and will be ever.

Yours as you know, M.R.

Elizabethan Prose Ed. Hanis, Longmans

Pickerill and Spurre: an inn. Substitute a more modern name if you wish.
groat: small silver coin of the time, then worth fourpence. Today . . .?

8 Sonnet (Fractured)

This poem, written during the First World War, describes the deaths of young soldiers in France and the reactions of those at home. It is a sonnet – that is, a fourteen line poem, often with a break between the first eight lines (octet) and the last six (sestet). Like many poems, this sonnet uses rhymes in a particular pattern. We can map out the rhyme pattern, or rhyme scheme, by giving the same letter to lines which rhyme with *each other*. The rhyme scheme for this sonnet is a b a b c d c d e f f e g g. Both the octet and the sestet begin with a question.

With this information, as well as using the sense, sounds, and beat of the various pieces below, put the sonnet together again.

Anthem For Doomed Youth
by Wilfred Owen (1893–1918)

1) but in their eyes
Shall shine the holy glimmers of good-byes.
2) The shrill, demented choirs of wailing shells
3) No mockeries now for them; no prayers or bells,
4) And each slow dusk a drawing-down of blinds.
5) What passing-bells for these who die as cattle?
Only the monstrous anger of the guns.
6) save the choirs,
7) What candles may be held to speed them all?
Not in the hands of boys
8) And bugles calling for them from sad shires.
9) Only the stuttering rifles' rapid rattle
10) The pallor of girls' brows
11) Nor any voice of mourning
12) Can patter out their hasty orisons.
13) shall be their pall;
Their flowers the tenderness of patient minds,

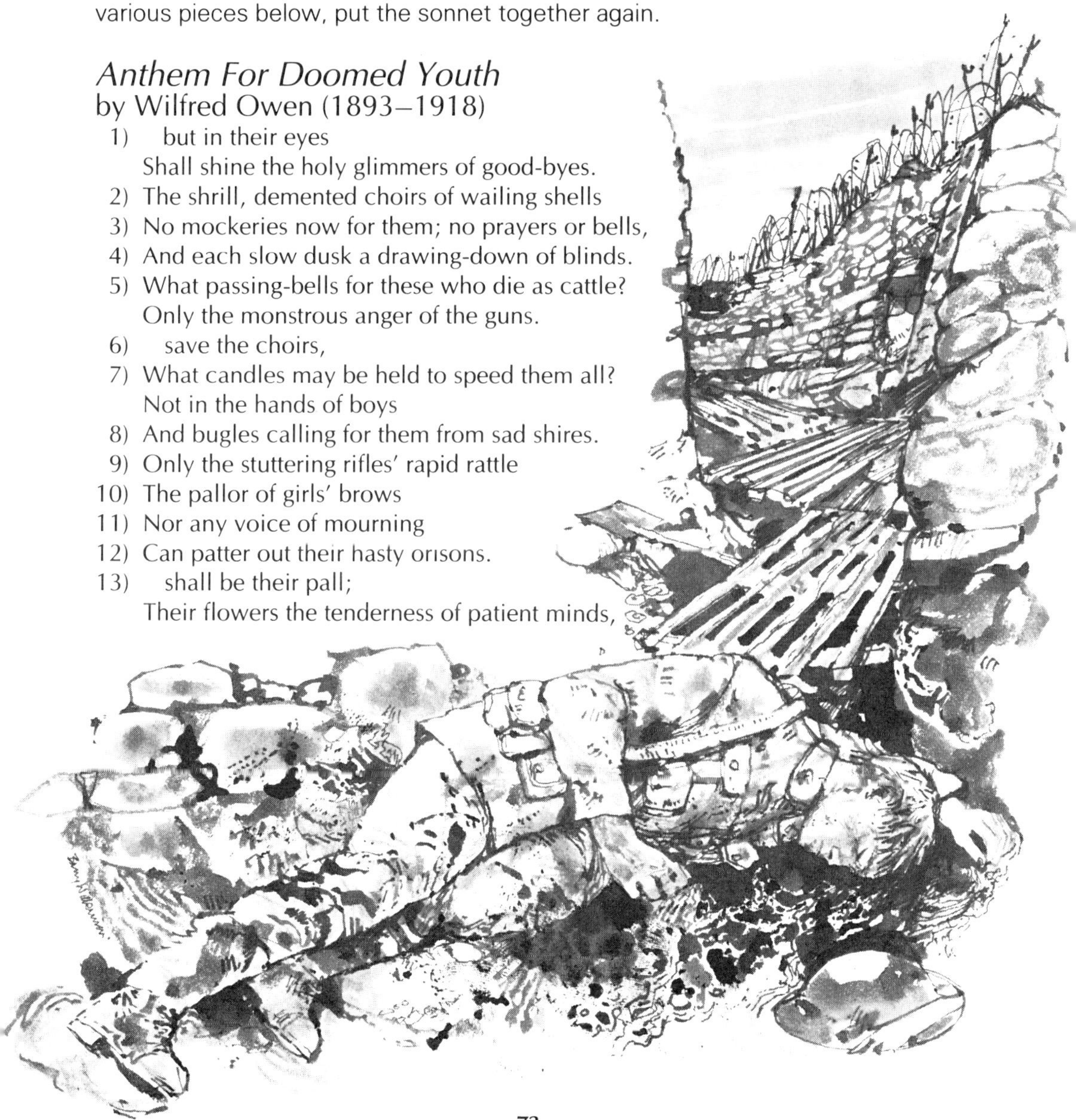

a) Now you've put the poem together, explain why you put the various bits where you did.
b) What do you notice about the ideas in the *octet* and those in the *sestet*? Why do you think the poet decided to break the sonnet there?
c) To what do "passing-bells", "orisons", "choirs" usually refer? Comment on why Owen uses these words here.
d) What mood (or moods) can you find in the poem? How does the poet create that particular mood?
e) Comment on the use of sounds in this poem. Select at least one example and say how sound is used by Owen.
f) Why do you think there's a change in the rhyme scheme between the octet and the sestet? What difference does it make?

Unit 3

For Discussion

Introduction

In this unit there are four passages which can be used for listening and/or discussion. It might be useful to have these passages taped by different speakers to give practice in listening to a range of voices. Of course, other passages in the book can also be used for listening and discussion if required.

It is usual to listen to the passage being read twice (on tape or by the teacher). During the first reading students can make notes without looking at the questions. They can look at the questions before and during the second reading.

1 The 'Mary Celeste' Mystery

Listen to the tape or the teacher. Do not start to answer the questions until the reading is over.

1. What do most people know about the story of the *Mary Celeste*? (3)
2. Nonetheless, 'very few seem to know the true facts of the case'. *In your own words*, explain why that is. (2)
3. Why does the speaker bother to say 'not *Marie Celeste*, by the way'? (1)
4. The following nautical terms are used in the passage, and their definitions are also given. Write the appropriate definition beside the word: Brigantine Spoke (2)
5. How many people in all were aboard the *Mary Celeste*? (1)
6. From the evidence of the extract, between what two dates did the people on board disappear? (2)
7. Who was the captain of the *Dei Gratia*? (1)
8. Was the *Dei Gratia* heading a) in the same direction as the *Mary Celeste*, or b) in the opposite direction? (1)
   Write down the *single word* that tells you this. (1)
9. Explain fully in your own words why the captain of the *Dei Gratia* found the *Mary Celeste*'s appearance surprising –
   a) at first sight, b) on closer inspection. (4)
10. How many men were sent to investigate? (1)
    How many went on board? (1)
11. What was the first thing they did? Why? (2)
12. What two things did they realise from their *initial* investigations? (2)
13. What suggested that the ship had been abandoned 'at a moment's notice'? Give *full* details. (4)
14. a) What very important point is generally overlooked? (1)
    b) What makes it very important? (1)

(30)

2 We Had Another Customer

Where you have to make a choice from a series of possible answers, you need only write the letter you think is appropriate.

1. The story is told by someone from:
   a) France b) Australia c) Ireland d) America e) Yorkshire. (1)
2. The action takes place in:
   a) the desert b) a farming area c) a small village d) a city e) unspoilt countryside. (1)
3. It takes place in about:
   a) 1914 b) 1842 c) 1940 d) 2055 e) 1899. (1)
   Give a reason for your answer. (1)
4. It takes place at:
   a) dawn b) mid-morning c) noon d) afternoon e) evening. (1)
5. a) Explain *fully* what the weather was like. (2)
   b) What effect did it have on people in general? (1)
   c) How does this fit into the story? (1)
6. What is the speaker's name? (1)
7. What details suggest the kid is inexperienced in his job? (2)
8. What is the speaker's attitude to the drunk's demands for a drink? (1)
9. What does the speaker mean by "Warner Brothers could use that"? (2)
10. In your own words, what does the kid's reply tell us? (1)
11. What kind of appearance (in the way he dressed) did the new customer have and what mood was he in? (2)
12. For what reason did the new customer come into the bar? (1)
13. What was it about the new arrival which the speaker didn't like? (1)
14. What was the victim's name? (1)
15. Write down the detail which tells us the victim had fallen heavily and lay very still. (1)
16. What does the speaker's reaction reveal about his personality when the drunk turns the gun on him? (1)
17. What details suggest the getaway was fast? (2)
18. What does the speaker's last remark mean? Explain *fully*. (2)
19. Choose one aspect of the *way* in which the incident is told.
    a) Say what it is. (1)
    b) Say what it tells us about the personality of the speaker. (1)
20. What kind of a story do you think this incident comes from? (1)

(30)

3 On Heavy Tibetan Boots

1. Explain **fully** how the hills contrast with the floor of the valley. (4)
2. a) In a sentence, state what was the disadvantage of the valley being so sheltered. (1)
   b) What made this effect worse? (2)
   c) In a sentence, state what other disadvantage the valley had. (1)
   d) What caused this? (1)
3. "Even the Dze Chu was all but frozen over."
   What does this tell you about the Dze Chu compared to the other streams? (1)
4. Where is the Dze La pass? How high is it? (2)
5. What was the weather like when they began the ascent of the Dze La? (Explain in your own words.) (2)
6. a) How did they find the climb towards the neck of the pass? (2)
   b) What made the last lap particularly difficult? (1)
7. What does the condition of their boots tell you about the travellers? (1)
8. What two effects did the east wind have on them? (2)
9. Write down the *single word* which tells you that the travellers were unwilling to turn back. (1)
10. In your own words explain how the descent the next day seemed to the travellers. (1)
11. a) What effect did their surroundings have on the travellers? (1)
    b) How does this valley differ from the one they were in before? (1)
12. How long did the journey in the passage take:
    a) a day b) two days c) three days d) four days? (1)
13. What, in your own words, is the Purdong Chu? (1)
14. a) In your own words, explain how they were going to cross the Purdong Chu. (1)
    b) Bearing in mind the way they were going to cross the Purdong Chu, explain fully and in your own words why they were going to cross it as early as possible the next morning, and not later in the day. (3)

(30)

4 Not Job

1. This incident takes place in:
   a) the University of Sandwich b) a government office c) a jam factory (1)
2. What is the 'Officer's' name? (1)
3. The officer works as:
   a) a policeman b) a psychologist c) a careers officer d) a driver (1)
4. His client is:
   a) a recent school-leaver b) an experienced workman c) a university student d) a cat burglar (1)
5. How does the officer react to his client when he first speaks and why? (2)
6. Pick out one expression from the officer's *first speech* which is out of place for the sort of job the officer claims he does. What does this expression tell you about his attitude to his client? (2)
7. How does the officer react when he hears what qualifications his client has? (1)
8. What do we learn about the client's school career? (1)
9. a) What three choices is the client offered? Which one does he reject straight away? (2)
   b) What reasons does he give for this? (2)
10. From *what* he says and *how* he says it, how do we know the client hasn't got a very clear idea of the sort of job he wants? (2)
11. a) What reason does the officer give when he says his client should join the police and what reason does the client give for rejecting this suggestion? (2)
    b) What does the client's account of being a cat burglar tell us about his *personality*? (2)
12. a) What job does the officer offer next? What does the choice of job tell you about his opinion of his client? (2)
    b) From what he says and how he says it, how does he suggest the *nature* of the job? (2)
13. What does the *writer* intend when he describes the pink form as "personal"? (1)
14. What does the officer's last remark tell us about his real attitude towards the client? (1)
15. Looking at the scene overall;
    a) What ideas do you think the author wants this scene to present?
    b) Identify **two** methods which the author uses to present his ideas.
    c) Give a reason why you find this scene successful or unsuccessful in presenting these ideas. (4)

(30)

1 The 'Mary Celeste' Mystery

I want to tell you a little, to-day, about what's generally known as 'the greatest mystery of the sea.' That, of course, is the story of the *Mary Celeste*.

Most people have heard something about her: many who've never even seen the sea have heard rumours, if nothing more, of a ship found abandoned on the high seas, in good order and with sail set – but *without a soul on board*, and with nothing to show what on earth had become of her crew. For all that, very few seem to know the true facts of the case, because there's so much fiction mixed up with them. So I think the best thing I can do is to start by giving you what's known of the facts – as they came out at the official inquiry at Gibraltar – and leave the discussion of them till later.

The *Mary Celeste* (not *Marie Celeste*, by the way) was a wooden brigantine – that is, a two-masted sailing-ship – built in Nova Scotia. She was quite small – only 236 tons burthen, and no more than 96 feet long. She left New York on 7th November 1872 bound for Genoa with a cargo of whale oil, fusel oil, and crude alcohol (which is much the same thing as methylated spirit). She carried a crew of seven – mate, bos'n, four seamen and a cook: and her captain and part-owner, Benjamin S. Briggs, an American, also brought with him his wife and his little daughter Sophia, aged two.

The *Mary Celeste* 'spoke' – that is, exchanged signals with – another ship two days later, in a position about 300 miles S.E. of New York; after that she doesn't seem to have been sighted again until the fifth of December, when the English brig *Dei Gratia*, under Captain Morehouse, bound from New York to Gibraltar and then about half-way between the Azores and the coast of Portugal, found herself slowly overhauling a small brigantine. As he drew nearer, Morehouse recognised her as the *Mary Celeste*. He and Capt. Briggs were old acquaintances – they'd dined together in New York before the *Mary Celeste* sailed – and he knew him for a smart seaman: yet there was his ship yawing to and fro, luffing up one minute and falling off the next and, of all things, sailing on the port tack with only a jib and foretopmast-staysail set – and those set to starboard! Putting his telescope on to her – by now, the ships weren't more than half a mile apart – he saw that there was no one at the wheel, or anywhere on deck. Closing her still further, he hailed – but got no answer. So he lowered a boat and sent Oliver Deveau, his first mate, with two hands to investigate.

Deveau and one of his men climbed on board. The ship seemed deserted, so the first thing they did was to sound the well. No, the *Mary Celeste* was in no danger of sinking – although she'd obviously been through heavy weather, for there was a lot of water between decks. Most of her sails were furled; but, besides the two she was carrying, two others had apparently been set, and had blown away. Search in the cabin and foc'sle showed that there was no one on board, dead or alive. Crew, captain, wife and little girl – all were gone, so it seemed, at a moment's notice, for all their belongings were still on board. The cabin was full of personal gear, including a trunkful of clothes belonging to Mrs. Briggs and the little girl: and in the foc'sle the missing crew had left behind them not only their sea-chests (containing everything they possessed in the world) but even their pipes and tobacco! Nothing at all seemed to be missing except the ship's papers (the register, manifest, bill of lading etc.) *and the ship's boat*, the latter a very important point which is generally overlooked.

From *A First Book of Modern Prose*, Cassell.

2 We Had Another Customer

There was a desert wind blowing that night. It was one of those hot dry Santa Anas that come down through the mountain passes and curl your hair and make your nerves jump and your skin itch. On nights like that every booze party ends in a fight. Meek little wives feel the edge of the carving knife and study their husbands' necks. Anything can happen. You can even get a full glass of beer at a cocktail lounge.

I was getting one in a flossy new place across the street from the apartment house where I lived. It had been open about a week and it wasn't doing any business. The kid behind the bar was in his early twenties and looked as if he had never had a drink in his life.

There was only one other customer, a souse on a bar stool with his back to the door. He had a pile of dimes stacked neatly in front of him, about two dollars' worth. He was drinking straight rye in small glasses and he was all by himself in a world of his own.

I sat further along the bar and got my glass of beer and said: 'You sure cut the clouds off them, buddy. I will say that for you.'

'We just opened up,' the kid said. 'We got to build up trade. Been in before, haven't you, mister?'

'Uh-huh.'

'Live around here?'

'In the Berglund Apartments across the street,' I said. 'And the name is John Dalmas.'

'Thanks, mister. Mine's Lew Petrolle.' He leaned close to me across the polished dark bar. 'Know that guy?'

'No.'

'He ought to go home, kind of. I ought to call a taxi and send him home. He's doing his next week's drinking too soon.'

'A night like this,' I said. 'Let him alone.'

'It's not good for him,' the kid said, scowling at me.

'Rye!' the drunk croaked, without looking up. He snapped his fingers so as not to disturb his pile of dimes by banging on the bar.

The kid looked at me and shrugged. 'Should I?''

'Whose stomach is it? Not mine.'

The kid poured him another straight rye and I think he doctored it with water down behind the bar because when he came up with it he looked as guilty as if he'd kicked his grandmother. The drunk paid no attention. He lifted two dimes off his pile with the exact care of a crack surgeon operating on a brain tumour.

The kid came back and put more beer in my glass. Outside the wind howled. Every once in a while it blew the stained-glass swing-door open a few inches. It was a heavy door.

The kid said: 'I don't like drunks in the first place and in the second place I don't like them getting drunk in here, and in the third place I don't like them in the first place.'

'Warner Brothers could use that,' I said.

'They did.'

Just then we had another customer. A car squeaked to a stop outside and the swinging door came open. A fellow came in who looked a little in a hurry. He held the door and ranged the place quickly with flat, shiny, dark eyes. He was well set up, dark, good-looking in a narrow-faced, tight-lipped way. His clothes were dark and a white handkerchief peeped coyly from his pocket and he looked cool as well as under a tension of some sort. I guessed it was the hot wind. I felt a bit the same myself only not cool.

He looked at the drunk's back. The drunk was playing checkers with his empty glasses. The new customer looked at me, then he looked along the line of half-booths at the other side of the place. They were all empty. He came on in – down past where the drunk sat swaying and muttering to himself – and spoke to the bar kid.

'Seen a lady in here, buddy? Tall, pretty, brown hair, in a print bolero jacket over a blue crepe silk dress. Wearing a wide-brimmed straw hat with a velvet band.' He had a tight voice I didn't like.

'No, sir. Nobody like that's been in,' the bar kid said.

'Thanks. Straight Scotch. Make it fast, will you?'

The kid gave it to him and the fellow paid and put the drink down in a gulp and started to go out. He took three or four steps and stopped, facing the drunk. The drunk was grinning. He swept a gun from somewhere so fast that it was just a blur coming out. He held it steady and he didn't look any drunker than I was. The tall dark guy stood quite still and then his head jerked back a little and then he was still again.

A car tore by outside. The drunk's gun was a .22 target automatic, with a large front sight. It made a couple of hard snaps and a little smoke curled – very little.

'So long, Waldo,' the drunk said.

Then he put the gun on the barman and me.

The dark guy took a week to fall down. He stumbled, caught himself, waved one arm, stumbled again. His hat fell off, and then he hit the floor with his face. After he hit it he might have been poured concrete for all the fuss he made.

The drunk slid down off the stool and scooped his dimes into a pocket and slid towards the door. He turned sideways, holding the gun across his body. I didn't have a gun. I hadn't thought I needed one to buy a glass of beer. The kid behind the bar didn't move or make the slightest sound.

The drunk felt the door lightly with his shoulder, keeping his eye on us, then pushed through it backwards. When it was wide a hard gust of air slammed in and lifted the hair of the man on the floor. The drunk said: 'Poor Waldo. I bet I made his nose bleed.'

The door swung shut. I started to rush it – from long practice in doing the wrong thing. In this case it didn't matter. The car outside let out a roar and when I got onto the sidewalk it was flicking a red smear of tail-light around the nearby corner. I got its licence number the way I got my first million.

3 On Heavy Tibetan Boots

The broad and beautiful valley was flanked by big hills whose reddish soil contrasted sharply with the flower-studded grasslands below them. Its floor was so sheltered that we suffered badly from the heat in the middle of the day; our thick woollen robes did not improve matters, nor did the heavy packs whose straps chafed our shoulders painfully. As soon as the sun set, on the other hand, the valley – which is over twelve thousand feet above sea-level – became bitterly cold.

On the evening of the second day we rounded a big spur of rock and found ourselves on the threshold of a deep gorge at the far end of which was the high pass which we should have to cross next day. In spite of a fire made of twigs, we slept badly. It froze hard, and by dawn all the little streams had been turned to ice; even the Dze Chu was all but frozen over. We began the ascent of the Dze La pass, which is the highest in Eastern Tibet and rises to some sixteen thousand feet. A light mist imposed a wintry pallor on the rays of the early sun.

It was midday when we emerged from the gorge and saw the neck of the pass above us, not very far away. We climbed slowly towards it, plodding painfully upwards over turf dotted with boulders and pockets of unmelted snow. We kept on having to stop to get our breath back. At last there was only a saddle of snow ahead of us; beyond it the narrow pass was outlined against the bright blue sky like the hind-sight of a rifle. This last lap of the climb was terribly hard going, for our heavy Tibetan boots, worn smooth and thin by many long marches, would not grip the frozen surface. But at three o'clock we reached the pass and, subsiding on a dry boulder for a long rest, ate some wads of *tsampa* which we had prepared before beginning the climb.

Meanwhile the east wind got up and chilled us to the bone; we were forced to retrace our steps to find shelter in the lee of the pass. Night was falling when we halted on a stony ledge, a place of unimaginable desolation. There were a few stunted shrubs there, so we were able to make a fire; but its heat was not enough to make us warm again.

Next morning we crossed the pass once more and began a descent which seemed interminable. Moving down the bottom of a wild and gloomy gorge in which, since the sun never shone there, snow and ice had a depressing air of permanence, we had the feeling of being trapped. About noon, however, we struck an important tributary of the Mekong; it is called the Purdong Chu and is really not so much a tributary as a source. The valley through which it ran – at an altitude of some fourteen thousand feet – was deep and narrow. We decided to ford it as early as possible on the following morning, while the night-frost still immobilised some of the water which, when the sun reached the snows above us, would increase the difficulties of a passage.

From *A Journey in Disguise* by Andre Migot

4 Not Job

OFFICER: The government goes to all the fuss to build this lovely building, houses us, staffs it with disqualified civil servants, we sit here with only two tea breaks a day waiting to serve the public, wanting to serve the public, willing to serve the public and yet you go and get a job through the newspaper columns. Like a lost budgie. But now you come whining to us. . . .

. . . Now look, lad. I'm here to help. To serve the public. I'm here to find youths careers. That's why I'm called Youth Careers Officer. I took a course in it. University Sandwich. I was trained in social psychology. I was trained in adolescent problems. So now, button your lip, this is my cubicle. Now, you want a job. What certificates you got?

HARRY: Certificates?

OFFICER: Mental certificates lad. Exams. G.C.E. C.S.E. D.D. Certificates. Qualifications.

HARRY: I've got me Bronze Medallion for Life Saving and me Tenderfoot in the Cubs.

OFFICER: Is that all?

HARRY: Yes.

OFFICER: So, all we need is a job in a forest, by a lake, saving lives. Did you get anything else?

HARRY: No.

OFFICER: What, did they not give you anything when you left?

HARRY: I was supposed to hand me P.E. kit in, but I kept it.

OFFICER: And that is the sum total of your academic career?

HARRY: Yes.

OFFICER: Well, we could put you to an apprenticeship, on the buildings or in a factory.

HARRY: Apprenticeship is no use. Takes you five years to learn what you could pick up in six months.

OFFICER: You don't want an apprenticeship.

HARRY: No, but I want Saturday afternoons off.

OFFICER: That leaves you with labouring, or semi-skilled.

HARRY: I don't want that.

OFFICER: What sort of thing would you like? Now think about it. I can wait. Take your time. I'm patient. I was trained in psychology and all the rest of it. What sort of job would you like?

HARRY: I would like a job with adventure. Like on the telly. Lots of thrills. Pioneering, life. Colour. Like the pictures. I was brought up on the pictures.

OFFICER: Would you like to try the Police, you've got the height?

HARRY: I don't like law and order. It usually picks on me. If anything, I would be a cat burglar. But I'm frightened of heights. I keep planning daring daylight robberies but when I get to the stage for shinning up the drainpipe, I can't do it.

OFFICER: Well, all we need to find you is a cat burgling job. Ground floors only. Now come on, come on. I may have done psychology, but I'm not Job. It'll have to be the last stage of a conveyor belt. You can be the human end of a mechanised system, how will that suit you? Like jam. Take jam. The fruit comes in at one end, and is skinned and stoned by a machine, then it is washed and cleaned in a machine, then it is mixed with sugar in a huge boiler, worked by a machine, then it runs off into jars by a machine process. The jars are lidded by a machine; then they are boxed by a machine, then they are all pushed on conveyor belts and pushed along to the loading bay by a machine; and there on the loading bay is you. Lifting them on to a lorry, the human end to a machine system, how would you like that?

HARRY: Have they got nothing to lift them on with?

OFFICER: The driver likes somebody to talk to. Now, I'll fill you in a pink form, look, it's quite personal. It has your number for filling; and I'll put your name on it though that's not really necessary, but it'll make you feel good. Now, run along, and present that. Say you're from me, Mr Baxter. They know me down there, I've sent them some good lads. And they keep coming back for more. I'd send my own son down there only the lorry driver wouldn't get on with him.

HARRY: I don't like the idea of a card.

OFFICER: You've got to have a card.

HARRY: How do I reach the place?

OFFICER: The address is on it, look.

HARRY: But how do I reach it?

OFFICER: Just step outside son, and ask a policeman. Every man to his job.

From *Zigger Zagger* by Peter Terson